This book is dedicated to all of the wonderful educators that I have had the distinct pleasure of working with over the years. You are the hardest-working, most creative, and most caring group of people that I have ever had the pleasure to know. You are the constant solvers of problems, the inspiring weavers of dreams, and the great jugglers of tasks. I am lucky to have worked alongside you all of these years and to call you my friends.

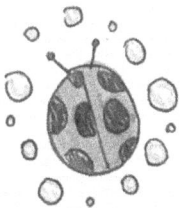

Buggy Bubbles Publishing
buggybubblespublishing.com

Book Cover by Jennifer Bowers

Illustrations by Jennifer Bowers and were AI-generated

First edition 2025

365 Days to Creativity: Fun Activities to Develop Creative Thinking Skills All Year Long

Written by Jennifer Bowers

Foreword

According to the late great E. Paul Torrance, often referred to as the Father of Creativity, "creativity is the highest form of mental functioning" and "creativity is the distinguishing characteristic of outstanding individuals in almost every field." I began my career of over thirty years in elementary education in the mid-1990s. We did not have computers in the classroom, and our curriculum was guided by textbooks and curriculum maps that we created during summer break. In 2001, I began teaching gifted students while pursuing my gifted certification. I instantly fell in love with the creativity involved in developing my own curriculum, providing the means for students to enhance their creativity, critical thinking, research skills, and communication skills while focusing on topics pertaining to Science and Social Studies.

In my over twenty years of teaching gifted students, so much has changed in the classroom and in society in general. Many students now have one-to-one devices at their disposal daily, and people are seldom seen out and about without a mini-computer on their person. People are not exercising necessary thinking skills as much, because they have become accustomed to the instant gratification of typing in a few keywords and receiving an answer within seconds. Children have become so accustomed to every minute of their day being structured by others that they struggle with the ability to generate ideas on their own and with the concept of risk-taking for fear of not having the "right" answer.

In a world where the future is uncertain and where people may struggle to find their place within it, it becomes more important than ever to develop and retain the humanistic qualities that cannot be replicated and that hold us together. In a world filled with AI, creativity is the only thing in which we humans excel. The ability to communicate with one another and to emotionally respond to others in an appropriate way allows us to solve problems effectively. The ability to collaborate with others, to remain resilient and flexible in the face of challenges, and to think creatively and critically allows us to generate new and exciting ways of doing things.

How to Use This Book

The structure of this book provides for a weekly theme and theme-related activities for each day that will exercise your creative thinking skills. Each activity is labeled as follows:

F: These activities can easily be enjoyed by families consisting of varying age levels. You could choose to make this part of a daily routine, such as family bonding time after dinner or part of the bedtime routine.

T: These activities are easily adaptable for use in a classroom setting. Teachers may choose to use these for warm-ups, early finishers, or curriculum enhancement to name a few.

C: These activities are well-suited for children to complete on their own either independently or with a group of friends, siblings, cousins, etc. These can be done during school breaks, free time, or waiting time (bus/car rides, waiting for appointments, etc.) to name a few examples.

As you will see, most activities can be utilized by multiple groups.

Feel free to do these in any order you wish. Life happens. Trust me, I know. My hope is that you will find this book to be a valuable tool for developing creative thinking skills as well as for providing some screen-free bonding time together. I hope that you make some lasting memories that you will cherish.

As Albert Einstein said, "Creativity is intelligence having fun." Indeed.

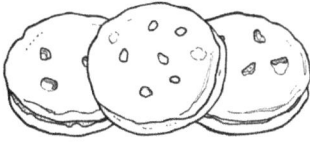

Day One: Fluency (F, T, C)

Task: Choose a central area to place a large piece of paper and use it to record as many types of cookies as you can think of. You may want to consider flavors, special occasions, ways to prepare, different cultures, and brands to name a few. Revisit the list as often as necessary throughout the day. How many did you brainstorm together?

Day Two: Figures of Speech (Idioms) (F, T, C)

Task: Cookies are frequently used in phrases to convey ideas. Some examples include:

- He/she is a smart cookie.
- He/she is a tough cookie.
- That's the way the cookie crumbles.
- He/she was caught with his/her hand in the cookie jar.
- All of the houses in the neighborhood are cookie-cutter houses.

While these phrases are not meant to be literal, what if they were? Can you draw a picture or create a story using one of these figures of speech in a literal way, such a highly-intelligent cookie? Or a cookie that was extremely hard or resilient?

Day Three: Combining (F, T, C)

Task: Can you combine a cookie with something completely unrelated to create something new? How would it work? Where could you use it? Who would use it? For example, you could combine a cookie with a car to create a Cookie Car! It would run on oven heat, and you could use it as long as the weather and ground were dry. The whole family could snack as you go, but it might need to be replaced frequently, depending on how hungry everyone is.

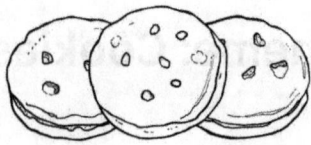

Day Four: Solving Problems (F, T, C)

Task: All day long, we encounter problems that must be solved. How could you use cookies to solve some of these common daily annoyances?

- Getting out of a traffic jam
- Getting caught unprepared in an unexpected rainstorm
- Running out of toilet paper in the bathroom

Day Five: Making Decisions Using Criteria (F, T)

Task: There are many different types of cookies in the world, but which one is the BEST? Each person is allowed one nomination to consider. How will you judge your nominees? What qualities of a cookie are most important to you? Is it chewiness? Is it sweetness? Is it how easy they are to bake? Is it the cost? Brainstorm 4-5 questions to consider when making your choice and make sure that you word your questions in a positive way. For example, if you like sweet cookies, your question might read, "Which is the sweetest?" If you are more health-conscious, your question might read, "Which is the healthiest?" Rate each cookie nomination for each of your questions using a smiley face (3 points) for "Definitely," a squiggly face (2 points) for "Sort Of," and a sad face (1 point) for "Not Really." Add up the points for each cookie to determine the winner. How will you decide a winner if there is a tie for first place?

Day Six: Originality (F, T)

Task: Brainstorm types of cookies that do not already exist, but they must be edible. How wild and crazy can you get? Choose one or more and bake a batch using an easy sugar cookie recipe or some purchased cookie dough. How were they? What changes would you make next time?

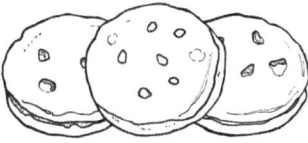

Day Seven: A Puzzling Situation (F, T, C)
Task: Look at the picture below. What do you suppose is going on here? What details do you notice in the picture? What questions do you have? What do you think happened? What do you think will happen next?

Week Two Theme: Dreams

Day One: Flexibility (F, T, C)
Task: Choose a central area and place a large piece of paper there. Think of as many TYPES of dreams as you can throughout the day. When you are done, try to brainstorm at least one example for each type you listed. For example, you may have listed DAYDREAM as a category, and one example of that could be winning the lottery. How many types did you come up with?

Day Two: Reflection (F, T, C)
Task: In many indigenous cultures, dreamcatchers are used to protect sleeping people from bad dreams. Suppose you could use a dreamcatcher during the daytime as well to capture other harmful things. What would you like to catch most? Why? Write a story or draw a picture to share with someone.

Day Three: Figures of Speech (Metaphors and Analogies) (F, T, C)
Task: How would you complete or explain the figures of speech below that are related to dreams? How many different responses can you brainstorm?

- A dream is like _____.
- A dream is a journey of the mind.
- Hopes and dreams are as powerful as _____.
- His/her head is in the clouds.
- A dream come true
- Beyond my wildest dreams

Week Two Theme: Dreams

Day Four: Put to a Different Use (F, T, C)

Task: Dreams help our brains by storing our memories, working through our feelings, and solving our problems. Can you think of something else that dreams could be useful for? Could you use your dreams to do tasks in real life? What if things that are not alive dreamed instead of living things? What would they dream about?

Day Five: Elaboration (F, T, C)

Task: Create a dream sequence by choosing a prompt below and adding more details as you move from person to the next. How elaborate can you get? How long can you keep the dream alive?

- Every night when I fall asleep, I have the same dream. The funny thing is, though, that the dream continues each night from where it left off the night before. It all started when...

- On the night of my thirteenth birthday, I fell asleep in my bedroom as I did most nights. As I drifted off to sleep, I suddenly heard a strange noise from under my bed...

- As I fell asleep, I could feel my bed sinking lower and lower until a sudden burst of sunlight woke me. Imagine my surprise to find myself in a forest surrounded by...

Week Two Theme: Dreams

Day Six: Symbolism (F, T, C)

Task: Everyone has hopes and dreams in life. What are yours? If you had to choose one or more symbols to represent the hopes and dreams that you have for your life, which ones would you choose from the list below? What do these symbols represent to you? Can you create any additional symbols on your own?

- Mountain
- Star
- Key
- Ladder
- Road
- Arrows
- Water
- Light
- Wings

Day Seven: Drawing Prompts (F, T, C)

Task: Copy the drawing prompt below onto a piece of plain paper. Using the subject "only in dreams," what can you draw while using the prompt as part of your picture? Can you include a background? What will you call your drawing?

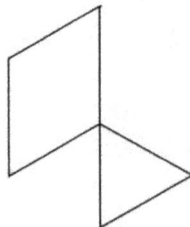

Week Three Theme: At the Zoo

Day One: Substitution (F, T, C)
Task: What body part or parts could you substitute with something else to make a zoo animal of your choice even better? For example, you could substitute a turtle's shell with a jet pack to make the turtle super fast and able to fly. How would you need to change the new zoo animal's habitat to make sure it was safe and happy?

Day Two: Humor (F, T, C)
Task: Can you use the prompts below to create jokes about zoo animals? How many different jokes can you make?

- Knock, knock. Who's there? Interrupting (choose a zoo animal). Interrupting (zoo animal) who? (Create a punchline!)
- Knock, knock. Who's there? (Choose a zoo animal) says. (Zoo animal) says who? (Create a punchline!)
- Why did the (choose a zoo animal) cross the road? (Create a punchline!)
- Why did the (choose a zoo animal) go to school? (Create a punchline!)
- I had a dream that I was a (choose a zoo animal). (Create a punchline!)
- A (choose a zoo animal) walked into a restaurant. (Create a punchline!)

Day Three: Fantasy (F, T, C)
Task: What do you think zoo animals talk about at night when people aren't around? Have each person choose the role of a zoo animal. Create a first-person dialogue imagining what you, as zoo animals, might talk about after hours. How long can you keep the conversation going?

Week Three Theme: At the Zoo

Day Four: Movement and Sound (F, T, C)
Task: Play a game of zoo animal charades by acting out an animal using movement and sound only. To make it more challenging, try it with ONLY movement or ONLY sound. Who is the champion?

Day Five: Emotions (F, T, C)
Task: How do you think zoo animals feel about the things happening in their lives? How can we know how they feel if we can't talk to them? How do they express emotions to us? Choose a situation below and explain how different animals might feel about it and express their feelings in it.

- Being enclosed in a zoo
- Being fed instead of capturing or finding food
- Being looked at by people all day
- Living in an artificial habitat instead of a natural one
- Having no predators

Day Six: Divergent and Convergent Thinking (F, T, C)
Task: Using small index cards or pieces of paper, brainstorm as many things as you can think of that you might see at a zoo. It could be anything, not just animals! Write each item on a separate card or piece of paper. After you have brainstormed as many as you can, how can you group these into categories? Which ones do you feel belong together? Why do they belong together? How many different ways can you come up with to group your words?

Week Three Theme: At the Zoo

Day Seven: A Puzzling Situation (F, T, C)

Task: Look at the picture below. What do you suppose is going on here? What details do you notice in the picture? What questions do you have? What do you think happened? What do you think will happen next?

Week Four Theme: Things That Fly

Day One: Observation (F, T, C)
Task: For the day, keep a journal or list of all of the things that you see that fly or are in some way related to the word "fly." At the end of the day, compare lists. Cross off any words or ideas that are identical. Who thought of the most original ideas?

Day Two: Aesthetic Thinking (F, T, C)
Task: Pretend that you had the ability to fly for just one day. Where would you go? What would you do? What would you see along the way? What would you hear on your journey? What new smells and tastes would you discover? What would it feel like?

Day Three: Missing Information (F, T, C)
Task: You are trying to decide whether to take an airplane for your next vacation. What information do you need to know in order to make the decision? How will you make the decision? What decision will you make?

Day Four: Lateral Thinking (F, T, C)
Task: One day, everything that flies suddenly stops simultaneously and floats slowly to the ground. What do you think might be going on? Why do you think that?

Week Four Theme: Things That Fly

Day Five: Direct Analogy (F, T, C)

Task: For each pair of words below, think of as many similarities as you can between the two words and as many differences as you can.

- Butterfly and Bed
- Airplane and Ice Cream
- Insect and Computer
- Bird and Football

Day Six: Brainstorming Solutions (F, T, C)

Task: You just spent weeks working together to construct a working model airplane. You take the airplane outside to try it out. It works! You take turns flying it around, but suddenly a burst of wind knocks it out of the sky. It comes crashing to the ground and breaks. How can you fix it using only materials that you already have so that it will fly again?

Week Four Theme: Things That Fly

Day Seven: Drawing Prompt (F, T, C)
Task: Copy the drawing prompt below onto a piece of plain paper. Using the subject "up, up, and away," what can you draw while using the prompt as part of your picture? Can you include a background? What will you call your drawing?

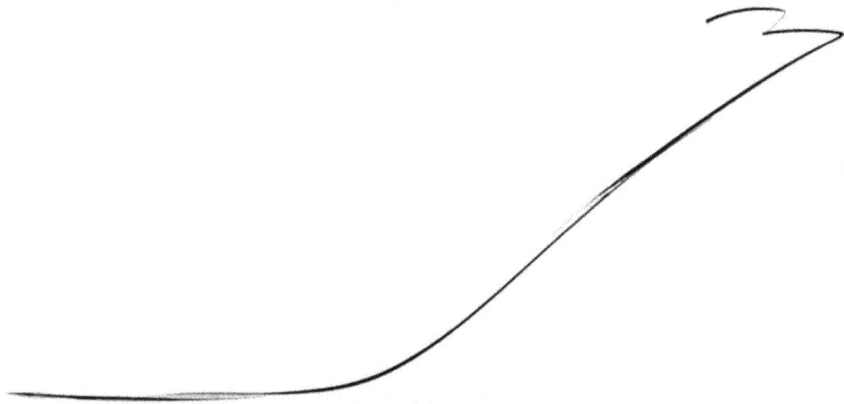

Week Five Theme: Music

Day One: Movement and Sound (F, T, C)

Task: Gather items around you that you can use to make different sounds. Some possibilities might be pots and pans, spoons (metal and wood), empty boxes, rubber bands, cardboard tubes filled with rice or pasta, empty jugs, glasses filled with different amounts of water, etc. Can you use your "instruments" to either create your own original songs or to play along with songs that you already know? Can you create some new dance moves to go along with it?

Day Two: Making Judgments (F, T, C)

Task: Looking at the statements below, do you think that they are true or false? Why?

- Everybody likes music.
- Music is a universal language in our world.
- It is easy to communicate emotions using music.
- Music reflects the beliefs and culture of people.
- Music helps our brains learn.

Day Three: Emotions (F, T, C)
Task: Can you think of or find examples of songs that could be used to represent all of the emotions below?

- Fear
- Happiness
- Excitement
- Sadness
- Anger
- Surprise
- Pride
- Love

Day Four: Oxymorons (F, T, C)
Task: Oxymorons are phrases that combine two opposite words to convey a new idea. How do you explain some of these oxymorons related to music? Can you think of some examples where you might encounter these?

- The Sound of Silence (Simon & Garfunkel)
- Break Up to Make Up (The Stylists and Ashanti)
- New, Old-fashioned Way (Brenda Lee's Rockin' Around the Christmas Tree)
- Hot 'n' Cold (Katy Perry)
- Cold Fire (Rush)
- Some of My Lies Are True (Huey Lewis & the News)
- Happy Sad (Rodney Allen)
- Act Naturally (Buck Owens)
- Bitter Sweet Symphony (The Verve)

Day Five: Rearrange (F, T, C)

Task: You found some old pieces of different musical instruments, and you have been trying to put them together to invent a brand-new instrument. The only problem is that it's not working very well right now. Can you rearrange the pieces so that it will work better?

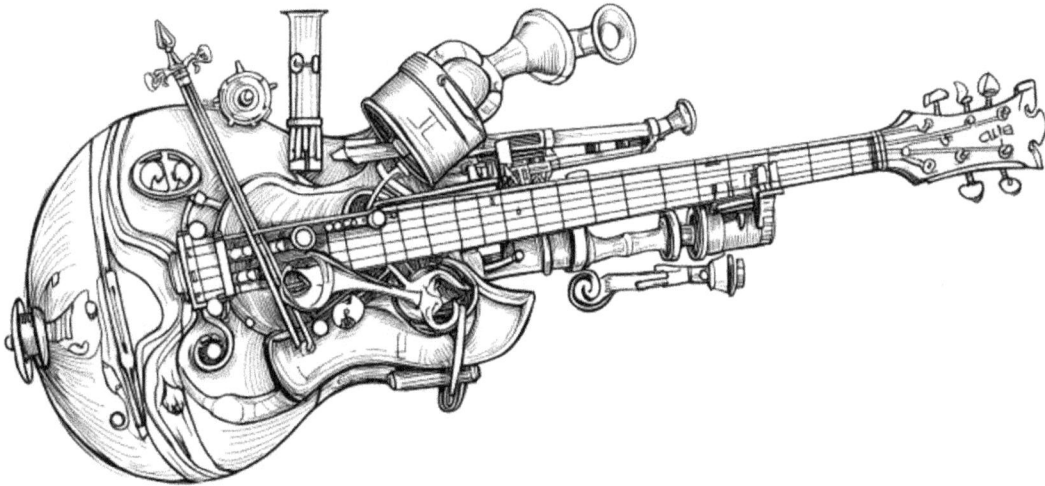

Day Six: Risk-taking (F)

Task: Find a place near you with a free or low-cost concert by looking up "free music shows near me." Try to find one that is at a place you have never been and/or that plays music that you don't usually listen to. Was it worth the risk? Would you try this again? Why or why not?

Day Seven: A Puzzling Situation (F, T, C)

Task: Look at the picture below. What do you suppose is going on here? What details do you notice in the picture? What questions do you have? What do you think happened? What do you think will happen next?

Week Six Theme: "Family"

Day One: Change Management (F)

Task: For part or all of one day, switch roles so that the grown-ups have to act like the kids and the kids have to act like adults. What will you need to do in your new role? How will you act? How will the things that need to be done in your household get done? Once you are done, discuss what you did and did not like about switching roles. Would you like to try this again? Maybe next time you would like to switch roles with a particular family member?

Day Two: Museum Walk (F, T, C)

Task: Have each person create a poster about themselves using pictures and phrases that best represent themselves. You can create these on your own or cut them out of a magazine. Hang the posters around the room. Have each person rotate to each poster and write/draw new items that they admire about each person. Feel free to come back to the posters throughout the day to add special memories, words of encouragement, and loving words for each person.

Week Six Theme: "Family"

Day Three: Mind Map (F, T, C)

Task: Using a model similar to the one below, create a mind map about family. Write the word "family" in the center circle and then think of some "big ideas" related to family to label the circles branching out from the center. You may use words and/or pictures to represent your ideas. Describe these big ideas further by connecting more circles and branches and labeling those with words and/or pictures. How detailed can you get?

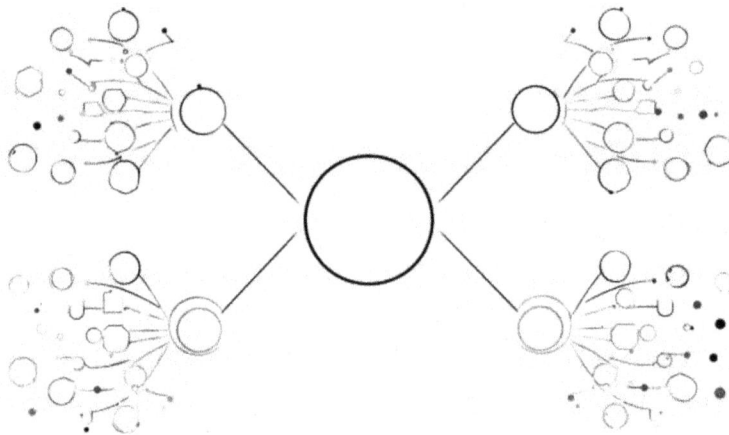

Day Four: Challenging Norms (F, C)

Tasks: Norms are simply the way that we usually do things. Every family is different and has their own ways of doing things. If you could challenge or change one or more of the family norms below, what would it be? Why?

- The way we communicate with each other
- Our daily routines
- Our responsibilities and rules
- Our traditions
- The way we make major family decisions

Week Six Theme: "Family"

Day Five: Design Thinking (F, T, C)

Task: Pair up with someone and interview each other about a problem that each of you is currently having. Brainstorm ideas to solve your partner's problem. Create an action plan or a model of an invention (does not need to be real) that would solve their problem. Present your solution to your partner and gather feedback. Make any modifications necessary and present your final idea.

Day Six: Social Activism (F, T, C)

Task: Decide which issues you care most about. Some ideas include animals, the environment, health, helping others in need, etc. What can you do to help your cause? Can you volunteer somewhere? Create a collection site? Do something in your own community? Put your care and concern into action!

Day Seven: Drawing Prompt (F, T, C)

Task: Copy the drawing prompt below onto a piece of plain paper. Using the subject "all in the family," what can you draw while using the prompt as part of your picture? Can you include a background? What will you call your drawing?

Week Seven Theme: Jobs

Day One: Negative Brainstorming (F, T, C)
Task: Brainstorm as many BAD examples as you can think of for jobs. For instance, professional nosepicker or professional paint-drying watcher might be some BAD examples of jobs.

Day Two: Pros and Cons (F, T, C)
Task: Make a list of all of the pros and cons you can think of for working at a job. How would your answers change depending upon the job you have? What are some pros and cons for NOT having a job? How might your answers change if money was not a worry for you?

Day Three: Perspectives (F, T, C)
Task: Think of a person who has a job that helps you in some way. What exactly do they do for you? Do you think they like doing the things they do for you and others? Why or why not? How might you treat this person differently now that you have looked at things from their perspective?

Week Seven Theme: Jobs

Day Four: Collaboration (F, T, C)

Task: Think of a big job in that you have been putting off. Collaborate together to get it done. First, come up with a plan to determine who will be responsible for which parts of the job to get the whole job done. Be prepared to adjust your plan if needed!

Day Five: Being Flexible (F, T, C)

Task: How would you get the jobs below done as you overcome each obstacle?

- How would you cook dinner if the electricity suddenly went out?
- How would you take a shower or bath when you run out of soap?
- How would you brush your teeth if you had to wear a full cast on the arm that you use to write with?
- How would you get your homework done if you suddenly found out that your entire afternoon and evening were completely filled with other obligations?

Day Six: Modify (F, T, C)

Task: How would the world be different if the tools that the people below use to do their jobs were suddenly MAGNIFIED (made much larger) or MINIMIZED (made much smaller)?

- Dentist
- Firefighter
- Actor/Actress
- Teacher
- Farmer

Week Seven Theme: Jobs

Day Seven: A Puzzling Situation (F, T, C)
Task: Look at the picture below. What do you suppose is going on here? What details do you notice in the picture? What questions do you have? What do you think happened? What do you think will happen next?

Week Eight Theme: Weather

Day One: Yes, and... (F, T, C)
Task: Using the prompt "My favorite weather is ____, because ____," take turns to complete the sentence. The next person should follow with "Yes, and...." in order to agree and add more details. Continue until everyone has contributed to the line of discussion. Then, someone else will take a turn to complete the prompt with a different type of weather, allowing others to follow with "Yes, and..." statements. How long can you keep the conversation going?

Day Two: Brainstorming Problems and Solutions (F, T, C)
Task: Think of a type of dangerous weather that is common for the area in which you live. Brainstorm potential problems that this weather could cause you. Then brainstorm possible solutions for each problem. Use the information to create an emergency preparedness kit and plan.

Day Three: Modify (F, T, C)
Task: Have you ever noticed that raincoats keep you mostly dry, but they don't keep you particularly warm or completely dry? Or that snowsuits keep you warm, but they don't keep you particularly dry and can be rather bulky? How can you modify either a raincoat or a snowsuit to make it just perfect?

Week Eight Theme: Weather

Day Four: Eliminate (F, T, C)
Task: If you could permanently eliminate one type of weather from the world, what would it be and why? What effect do you think this would have on the rest of the world?

Day Five: Personal Analogy (F, T, C)
Task: Pretend that you are either a raindrop or a snowflake. Write a song, story, or poem in the first person about your experiences.

Day Six: Curiosity (F, T, C)
Task: Brainstorm as many questions as you can think of about the weather. Use some of the question stems below to help you. What answers can you come up with?

- Who? What? Where? When? Why? How?
- What if?
- Why is _____ important?
- How would things be different if?

Week Eight Theme: Weather

Day Seven: Drawing Prompt (F, T, C)

Task: Copy the drawing prompt below onto a piece of plain paper. Using the subject "under the weather," what can you draw while using the prompt as part of your picture? Can you include a background? What will you call your drawing?

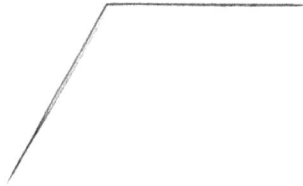

Week Nine Theme: Time

Day One: Figures of Speech (Idioms) (F, T, C)
Task: Time is frequently used in phrases to convey ideas. Some examples include:

- Beat the clock
- In the nick of time
- Time flies
- On borrowed time
- Time is money

While these phrases are not meant to be literal, what if they were? Can you draw a picture or create a story using one of these figures of speech in a literal way?

Day Two: Abstract Thinking (F, T, C)
Task: Do you think that time is most like a lasagna, a spring, or an arrow? Why?

Day Three: Experimentation (F, T, C)
Task: Make a prediction about how many times you can do each of the following tasks in one minute. Then, test out your theory. Was your prediction correct? What adjustments can you make to your experiment to change your outcomes?

- Flip a coin
- Do a jumping jack
- Tie your shoe
- Write your full name

Week Nine Theme: Time

Day Four: Making Decisions Using Criteria (F, T)

Task: There are many different ways that you could spend your time today, but how will you decide? Each person is allowed one nomination to consider. How will you judge your nominees? What is most important to you? Is it fun? Is it wisdom? Is it cost? Brainstorm 4-5 questions to consider when making your choice and make sure that you word your questions in a positive way. For example, if you like fun, your question might read, "Which is the most fun?" If you are more concerned about spending time wisely, your question might read, "Which is the wisest?" Rate each nomination for each of your questions using a smiley face (3 points) for "Definitely," a squiggly face (2 points) for "Sort Of," and a sad face (1 point) for "Not Really." Add up the points for each nominee to determine the winner. How will you decide a winner if there is a tie for first place?

Day Five: Internal Visualization (F, T, C)

Task: If you could shrink yourself and go inside a clock or watch, what do you think you would see? What would you do?

Day Six: Fantasy (F, T, C)

Task: If you could travel in time (forward or backward), WHEN and WHERE would you go? WHO would you meet? WHAT would you do? WHY did you make the choice that you did?

Week Nine Theme: Time

Day Seven: A Puzzling Situation (F, T, C)

Task: Look at the picture below. What do you suppose is going on here? What details do you notice in the picture? What questions do you have? What do you think happened? What do you think will happen next?

Week Ten Theme: Television

Day One: Divergent and Convergent Thinking Skills (F, T, C)

Task: Using small index cards or pieces of paper, brainstorm as many things as you can think of that are associated with television. It could be anything! Write each item on a separate card or piece of paper. After you have brainstormed as many as you can, how can you group these into categories? Which ones do you feel belong together? Why do they belong together? How many different ways can you come up with to group your words?

Day Two: Making Judgments (F, T, C)

Task: Looking at the statements below, do you think that they are true or false? Why?

- Television has a bad effect on people's health.
- Everyone likes to watch television.
- Watching television has educational value.
- The programs on television are quality entertainment.
- Watching television keeps people informed about what is happening in the world.

Day Three: Adapt (F, T, C)

Task: Can you brainstorm ideas so that watching television is a more immersive experience? How can you make changes so that you really feel like you are part of the show? Can you borrow ideas from other products? How could you incorporate the processes of sight, sound, touch, smell, and taste?

Week Ten Theme: Television

Day Four: Emotions (F, T, C)
Task: Can you think of or find examples of TV moments that could be used to represent all of the emotions below?

- Happiness
- Sadness
- Excitement
- Confusion
- Anger
- Nervousness

Day Five: Figures of Speech (Metaphors and Analogies) (F, T, C)
Task: How would you complete or explain the figures of speech below that are related to television? How many different responses can you brainstorm?

- Television is like ____.
- A television is as bright as ____.
- Television is ____ for the eyes.
- She is a couch ____.
- When I was your age, television was called ____.

Day Six: Combining (F, T, C)
Task: Can you combine two television shows together to create something new? How would it work? Who would be the main characters and where/when would the show take place? What would be the main plot of the new show?

Week Ten Theme: Television

Day Seven: Drawing Prompt (F, T, C)

Task: Copy the drawing prompt below onto a piece of plain paper. Using the subject "what's on tonight," what can you draw while using the prompt as part of your picture? Can you include a background? What will you call your drawing?

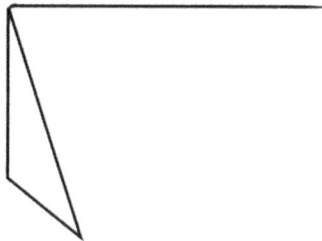

Week Eleven Theme: Outer Space

Day One: Oxymorons (F, T, C)
Task: Oxymorons are phrases that combine two opposite words to convey a new idea. How do you explain some of these oxymorons related to space? Can you think of some examples where you might encounter these?

- Darkness visible
- Loud silence
- Lonely crowd
- Empty fullness
- Dark brightness
- Controlled chaos
- Expensive affordability
- Limited infinity
- Isolated connectivity

Day Two: Fluency (F, T, C)
Task: Choose a central area to place a large piece of paper and use it to record as many things associated with outer space as you can think of. Revisit the list as often as necessary throughout the day. How many did you brainstorm together? Was it more or less than the last time you brainstormed a list like this?

Week Eleven Theme: Outer Space

Day Three: Challenging Norms (F, T, C)

Task: There are some things that are generally considered to be unwritten guidelines about space. If you could challenge or change one or more of the space norms below, what would it be? Why?

- People should avoid leaving debris in outer space.
- People should share their spacecraft locations with others to avoid collision.
- People should use the moon and other bodies in space only for peaceful purposes.
- Space should be free for anyone to explore.
- People should cooperate with others in order to explore space.
- The purpose of space exploration should be to benefit all of mankind.

Day Four: Fantasy (F, T, C)

Task: Pretend that you woke up one day to find an alien standing at the foot of your bed looking at you. What would you do? How would you feel? What would you say? How do you think the alien got there? What do you think the alien wants? What do you think would happen?

Week Eleven Theme: Outer Space

Day Five: Humor (F, T, C)
Task: Use the sentence stems below to create jokes related in some way to outer space.

- Why did _____ go to school?
- What kind of music _____?
- Why did _____ go to space?
- What did the _____ say to _____?
- Where would _____ park his/her/its spaceship?
- What was the first _____ in space?
- Why did the _____ cross the solar system?

Day Six: Role-Playing (F, T, C)
Task: Create and act out a skit about a spacecraft blast off. Who will play each role and what will their jobs be during the countdown? What will each person say? What costumes and props will you incorporate into your skit? What might go wrong during the countdown? How will you solve the problem?

Week Eleven Theme: Outer Space

Day Seven: A Puzzling Situation (F, T, C)
Task: Look at the picture below. What do you suppose is going on here? What details do you notice in the picture? What questions do you have? What do you think happened? What do you think will happen next?

Week Twelve Theme: Comfort

Day One: Movement and Sound (F, T, C)
Task: Take some time today to reflect about the movements and sounds that bring you comfort. Create a list so that you can use these the next time you need some comfort. Also, take some time to reflect about the things that do NOT bring you comfort. Create a list so that you can avoid these as needed in the future.

Day Two: Risk-Taking (F, T, C)
Task: Try something new today that you have been too afraid to try so that you are working OUTSIDE of your comfort zone. Is it meeting someone new? Is it speaking in front of a group of people? Is it coming into close contact with something that is not dangerous but still scary for you? See if you can overcome one of your fears (or at least become a bit more comfortable with it) today.

Day Three: Perspectives (F, T, C)
Task: How do you think the idea of comfort changes depending on factors, such as your age or circumstances? What things might bring the following groups below comfort?

- Babies
- Children
- Teenagers
- Adults
- Animals
- People experiencing illness or injury
- People experiencing a recent life-changing event

How might you bring comfort to one of these groups today?

Week Twelve Theme: Comfort

Day Four: Abstract Thinking (F, T, C)

Task: If you could choose a shape to be the mascot of "comfort," what shape would you choose? Would it be a circle, square, rectangle, triangle, oval, star, or pentagon? Why would you choose that shape? Use the shape to create an official mascot for "comfort."

Day Five: Put to a Different Use (F, T, C)

Task: Many people use items, such as a blanket, for comfort. How many different uses can you think of for a blanket BESIDES comfort and warmth?

Day Six: Rearrange (F, T, C)

Task: Can you rearrange the bedroom below so that it is as comfortable as possible? What items might you add to make it even more comfortable? Draw a sketch of the new and improved bedroom.

Week Twelve Theme: Comfort

Day Seven: Drawing Prompt (F, T, C)
Task: Copy the drawing prompt below onto a piece of plain paper. Using the subject "warm and cozy," what can you draw while using the prompt as part of your picture? Can you include a background? What will you call your drawing?

Week Thirteen Theme: On the Playground

Day One: Design Thinking (F, T, C)

Task: Household pets, such as cats and dogs, are at a significant risk of being obese because of lack of exercise. This puts them at risk for many health problems, such as diabetes, heart disease, joint problems, and respiratory problems to name a few. Can you design a playground specifically for dogs and/or cats so that they can get some needed exercise while having fun? The playground can either be for a public park or for an owner's backyard. What equipment will you have that will be able to be used by animals instead of people? Create a 2-D sketch or a 3-D model of your idea.

Day Two: Problem Solving (F, T, C)

Task: Your local park playground has become overgrown, unsafe, and unclean. How can you solve the problems that you see on the playground so that it is more fun for different age groups, safe for everyone, and clean? What will your new playground look like?

Week Thirteen Theme: On the Playground

Day Three: Direct Analogy (F, T, C)
Task: In what ways are a playground and a ceiling fan similar? In what ways are they different? Try to think of as many examples as possible.

Day Four: Making Decisions Using Criteria (F, T)
Task: Pretend that your family, local park, or school is considering installing a new piece of playground equipment. There is only enough money and space to purchase and install one. How will you decide what to choose? Each person should select one type of playground equipment. How will you judge your nominees? What qualities of playground equipment are most important to you? Is it safety? Is it how fun it is? Is it how easily different age groups can play on it? Brainstorm 4-5 questions to consider when making your choice and make sure that you word your questions in a positive way. For example, if you value safety, your question might read, "Which is the safest?" If you have children of different ages, your question might read, "Which one can be used by children of many ages?" Rate each nomination for each of your questions using a smiley face (3 points) for "Definitely," a squiggly face (2 points) for "Sort Of," and a sad face (1 point) for "Not Really." Add up the points for each piece of equipment to determine the winner. How will you decide a winner if there is a tie for first place?

Week Thirteen Theme: On the Playground

Day Five: Lateral Thinking (F, T, C)

Task: Pretend that you arrive at the park one day and find that there are only adults playing on the playground while the children are supervising them. In fact, as you look around, you suddenly notice that children are doing all of the "adult" things and adults are doing all of the "children" things. You see a car drive by with a little girl driving, and a crying man strapped in the car seat in the back. You look at the grocery store parking lot next door and see a little boy pushing the cart with a grown woman sitting in it. What do you think is going on here? Why?

Day Six: Changing Management (F)

Task: Kids, you're in charge today! Plan a family outing to a park, which includes a picnic. Pack a lunch for the family and be sure to bring any items that you may need to have for the outing, such as sunscreen, bug spray, etc.

Week Thirteen Theme: On the Playground

Day Seven: A Puzzling Situation (F, T, C)
Task: Look at the picture below. What do you suppose is going on here? What details do you notice in the picture? What questions do you have? What do you think happened? What do you think will happen next?

Week Fourteen Theme: Travel

Day One: Mind Map (F, T, C)

Task: Using a model similar to the one below, create a mind map about a dream vacation. Write the words "dream vacation" in the center circle and then think of some "big ideas" related to your dream vacation to label the circles branching out from the center. You may use words and/or pictures to represent your ideas. Describe these big ideas further by connecting more circles and branches and labeling those with words and/or pictures. You may want to visit your library to do some research on the place you'd like to visit for ideas. How detailed can you get?

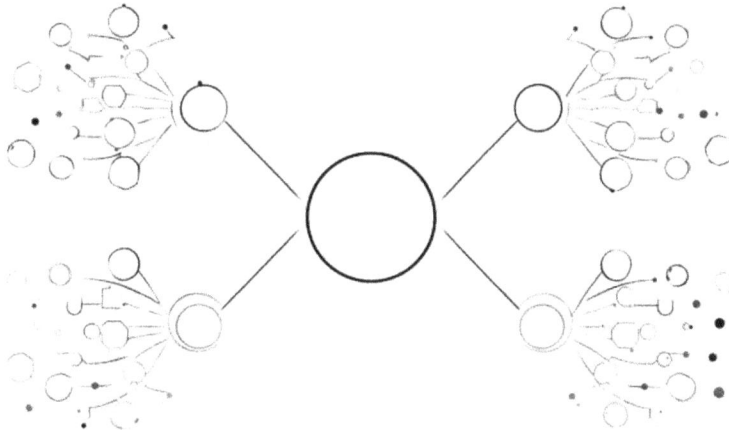

Day Two: Combining (F, T, C)

Task: Can you combine a car with something completely unrelated to create something new? You may choose to focus on making it more comfortable, faster, etc. How would it work? Where could you use it? Who would use it? Create a sketch of your new invention and explain how it works. What creative name will you give it?

Week Fourteen Theme: Travel

Day Three: Personal Analogy (F, T, C)
Task: Pretend that you are a car tire. Write a song, story, or poem in the first person about your experiences.

Day Four: Internal Visualization (F, T, C)
Task: If you could go inside the parts of an airplane that passengers don't normally go into, what do you think you would see? What would you do?

Day Five: Negative Brainstorming (F, T, C)
Task: Brainstorm as many BAD examples as you can think of for ways that you would NOT want to travel. For instance, traveling by porcupine-back or in a skunk-drawn wagon might be some BAD examples of ways to travel.

Day Six: Active Listening (F, T, C)
Task: If you could go anywhere, where would it be? Practice active listening by discussing this. The first person states their answer and a reason for it. The next person can choose to either agree or disagree respectfully by restating what the first person said and then stating their answer. Follow this format for the remainder of the discussion. How long can you keep the conversation going?

Week Fourteen Theme: Travel

Day Seven: Drawing Prompt (F, T, C)

Task: Copy the drawing prompt below onto a piece of plain paper. Using the subject "on the road again," what can you draw while using the prompt as part of your picture? Can you include a background? What will you call your drawing?

Week Fifteen Theme: Spring

Day One: Substitution (F, T, C)
Task: What parts of a flower could you substitute with something else to make a flower of your choice even better? How would your new and improved flower still get what it needs to survive?

Day Two: Observation (F, T, C)
Task: For the day, keep a journal or list of all of the things that you see, smell, taste, touch, and hear during spring. At the end of the day, compare lists. Cross off any words or ideas that are identical. Who thought of the most original ideas?

Day Three: Lateral Thinking (F, T, C)
Task: Pretend that everyone woke up one day, and all of the plants in a particular place had died overnight with no unusual weather. What do you think might be going on? What might happen next?

Day Four: Put to a Different Use (F, T, C)
Task: How many different uses can you think of for a spring?

Day Five: Eliminate (F, T, C)
Task: If you could permanently eliminate one thing about spring, what would it be? Why? What effect do you think it would have on the rest of the world?

Week Fifteen Theme: Spring

Day Six: Reflection (F, T, C)
Task: Spring is often symbolic of rebirth, new life, and progress. How can you carry these into your personal life? Are you going to try something new? Are you going to start doing something again that you haven't done in a long time? Are you going to set a new goal for yourself?

Day Seven: A Puzzling Situation (F, T, C)
Task: Look at the picture below. What do you suppose is going on here? What details do you notice in the picture? What questions do you have? What do you think happened? What do you think will happen next?

Week Sixteen Theme: In the City

Day One: Yes, and... (F, T, C)
Task: Using the prompt "If I could go to the city today, I would_____," take turns to complete the sentence. The next person should follow with "Yes, and...." in order to agree and add more details. Continue until everyone has contributed to the line of discussion. Then, someone else will take a turn to complete the prompt with a different answer, allowing others to follow with "Yes, and..." statements. How long can you keep the conversation going?

Day Two: Flexibility (F, T, C)
Task: Choose a central area and place a large piece of paper there. Think of as many TYPES of buildings as you can throughout the day. When you are done, try to brainstorm at least one example for each type you listed. How many types did you come up with?

Day Three: Pros and Cons (F, T, C)
Task: Make a list of all of the pros and cons you can think of for living in the city. How would your answers change depending upon which city you live in? What are some pros and cons for NOT living in the city? How might your answers change depending on where you live?

Week Sixteen Theme: In the City

Day Four: Experimentation (F, T, C)

Task: Using materials found around you, create a building challenge. Some materials might be paper, cardboard, craft sticks, straws, building blocks, tape, glue, rubber bands, string, marshmallows, spaghetti noodles, paper or plastic cups, egg cartons, aluminum foil, toothpicks, etc. First, decide whether you want to work individually or in teams. Then, decide on a goal for the challenge. Will you make buildings with a certain purpose? Or a certain strength? Or a certain height? Then, decide on the parameters. Will everyone have the same amount of materials? Will there be a time limit? Then, decide on how you will choose the winner. Will there be impartial judges? Will each building be put to a certain test? Conduct your challenge and determine a winner. If each person could change something about their design next time, what would it be?

Day Five: Social Activism (F, T)

Task: Investigate areas in which your city needs help. Some ideas might be to improve public spaces, support community services, volunteering at a food pantry, or volunteering at a youth organization. What can you do to help? Put your care and concern into action!

Week Sixteen Theme: In the City

Day Six: Oxymorons (F, T, C)
Task: Oxymorons are phrases that combine two opposite words to convey a new idea. How do you explain some of these oxymorons related to cities? Can you think of some examples where you might encounter these?

- Sustainable city
- Living in a ghost town
- Organized chaos
- Peaceful conflict
- Going nowhere fast
- Urban forest

Day Seven: Drawing Prompt (F, T, C)
Task: Copy the drawing prompt below onto a piece of plain paper. Using the subject "city that never sleeps," what can you draw while using the prompt as part of your picture? Can you include a background? What will you call your drawing?

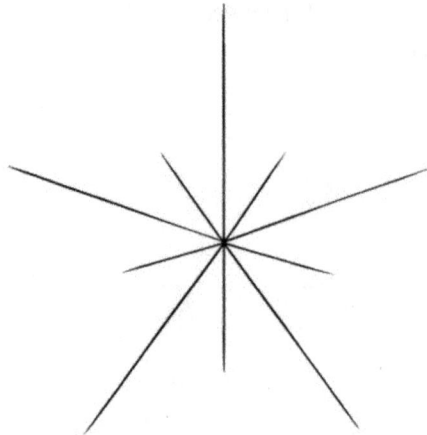

Week Seventeen Theme: Colors

Day One: Lateral Thinking (F, T, C)
Task: Suppose that you woke up one day and the entire world was black and white with no colors at all! No one else seems to notice anything is different. What do you think might be going on? Why do you think that?

Day Two: Reflection (F, T, C)
Task: It is said that younger people tend to dream in color and older people tend to dream in black and white. Do you think this is true? Why or why not? Do you dream in color or in black and white? What do you think this says about you?

Day Three: Originality (F, T, C)
Task: Great news! You have been chosen to create a new 8-pack of crayons with brand new colors. Your crayon pack must have a theme, and all of the names of the new colors should incorporate the theme. What will you create that does not already exist?

Day Four: Abstract Thinking (F, T, C)
Task: Many times, we use colors to communicate ideas without using any words or pictures. A traffic light is a good example of this. What do you think different colors are trying to communicate to us?

Week Seventeen Theme: Colors

Day Five: Movement and Sound (F, T, C)

Task: Have a color song dance party! Think of as many songs as you can think of to listen and dance to. Some ideas might include:

- "Blue Moon" by The Marcels
- "Yellow Submarine" by The Beatles
- "Orange Crush" by R.E.M.
- "Lady in Red" by Chris de Burgh
- "Black or White" by Michael Jackson
- "Purple Rain" by Prince
- "White Wedding" by Billy Idol
- "True Colors" by Cyndi Lauper

Day Six: Adapt (F, T, C)

Task: Can you brainstorm ideas so that colors are a more immersive experience? How could you incorporate sight, sound, touch, smell, and taste?

Week Seventeen Theme: Colors

Day Seven: A Puzzling Situation (F, T, C)
Task: Look at the picture below. What do you suppose is going on here? What details do you notice in the picture? What questions do you have? What do you think happened? What do you think will happen next?

Week Eighteen Theme: Toys & Games

Day One: Combining (F, T, C)
Task: Can you combine two toys together to create something new? How would it work? Who would most likely enjoy playing with it?

Day Two: Design Thinking (F, T, C)
Task: A big problem today is too much screen time. Can you design a new game or toy for families to play with together that involves no screen time while having fun? How will it work? Create a 2D sketch or a 3D model of your idea.

Day Three: Making Decisions Using Criteria (F, T)
Task: There are many different toys and games in the world, but which one is the BEST? Each person is allowed one nomination to consider. How will you judge your nominees? What qualities of a toy or game are most important to you? Is it amount of fun? Is it the challenge? Is it how easy it is to play? Is it the cost? Brainstorm 4-5 questions to consider when making your choice and make sure that you word your questions in a positive way. For example, if you like fun, your question might read, "Which is the most fun?" If you like challenge, your question might read, "Which is the most challenging?" Rate each nomination for each of your questions using a smiley face (3 points) for "Definitely," a squiggly face (2 points) for "Sort Of," and a sad face (1 point) for "Not Really." Add up the points for each toy or game to determine the winner. How will you decide a winner if there is a tie for first place?

Week Eighteen Theme: Toys & Games

Day Four: Brainstorming Solutions (F, T, C)
Task: You are stuck outside for the afternoon with your friend, and the only thing you have to play with is a ball. What can you do with the ball aside from the usual bouncing, kicking, and throwing to have some fun? If you could change the ball in some way to make it more fun, what would you do?

Day Five: Divergent and Convergent Thinking (F, T, C)
Task: Using small index cards or pieces of paper, brainstorm as many things as you can think of that are associated with toys and games. Write each item on a separate card or piece of paper. After you have brainstormed as many as you can, how can you group these into categories? Which ones do you feel belong together? Why do they belong together? How many different ways can you come up with to group your words?

Day Six: Experimentation (F, T)
Task: Make some play dough today using a simple homemade recipe that you already have or that you look up online. Experiment with different colors and scents. What can you build? Use your imagination!

Day Seven: Drawing Prompt (F, T, C)

Task: Copy the drawing prompt below onto a piece of plain paper. Using the subject "fun in the sun," what can you draw while using the prompt as part of your picture? Can you include a background? What will you call your drawing?

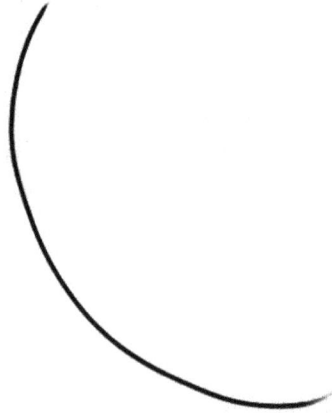

Week Nineteen Theme: Myths & Magic

Day One: Originality (F, T, C)
Task: What are some things that you would like to get done in a quicker, easier way? What are some things that you wish you could do but can't? Create some magic spells to get them done! What will the name of the spells be? What magic words would you include?

Day Two: Fantasy (F, T, C)
Task: Imagine that you arrive at work or school one morning to find that one or more mythical characters from the past have just transferred to your class or workplace. Create a story (oral or written) to explain what their first day would be like.

Day Three: Modify (F, T, C)
Task: Think of an existing mythical or magical character. Now, magnify (make larger) or minimize (make smaller) some of their features, powers, and tools. What would your new character be like? Draw a diagram of your new character, explaining the changes. Would you character need a new name? What would it be?

Week Nineteen Theme: Myths & Magic

Day Four: Mind Map (F, T, C)

Task: Using a model similar to the one below, create a mind map about a brand new national holiday to honor myths and magic. Write the name of your new holiday in the center circle and then think of some "big ideas" related to the new holiday (ceremonies, special events, foods, etc.) to label the circles branching out from the center. You may use words and/or pictures to represent your ideas. Describe these big ideas further by connecting more circles and branches and labeling those with words and/or pictures. How detailed can you get?

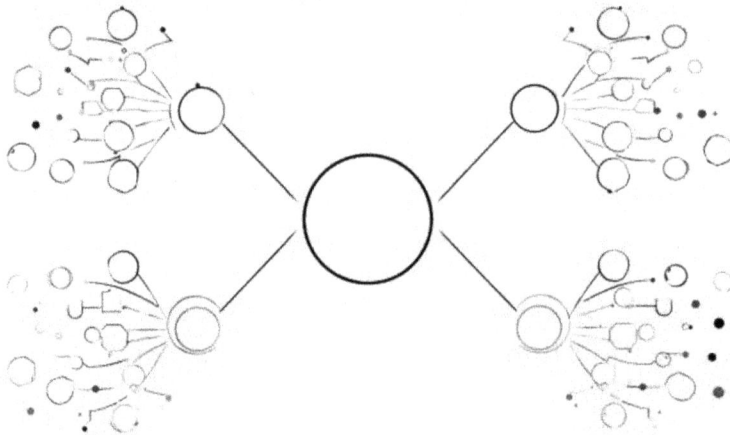

Week Nineteen Theme: Myths & Magic

Day Five: Challenging Norms (F, T, C)

Tasks: Norms are simply the way that we usually do things. If you could challenge or change one or more of the norms associated with myths and magic below, what would it be? Why?

- Characters who are too proud of themselves always have a downfall in the end.
- There are types of magic that should never be used.
- The greater the spell, the more power it needs.
- Magic should not be used in front of people who are not magical.
- Characters who are kind, honest, and patient will be rewarded in the end.
- Characters who do not obey or do the right thing will be punished.

Day Six: Fluency (F, T, C)

Task: Choose a central area to place a large piece of paper and use it to record as many things associated with myths and magic as you can think of. Revisit the list as often as necessary throughout the day. How many did you brainstorm together? Was it more or less than the last time you brainstormed a list like this?

Week Nineteen Theme: Myths & Magic

Day Seven: A Puzzling Situation (F, T, C)

Task: Look at the picture below. What do you suppose is going on here? What details do you notice in the picture? What questions do you have? What do you think happened? What do you think will happen next?

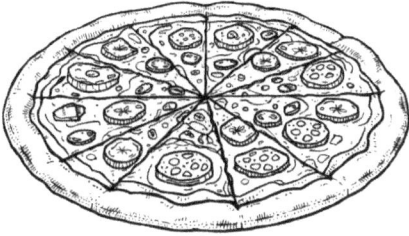

Week Twenty Theme: Pizza

Day One: Symbolism (F, T, C)
Task: Think of the different shapes associated with pizza-the different toppings, the way it's cut, etc. Now, think of what else those shapes could be used to represent. What is the craziest type of pizza that you can think of by substituting symbols for these shapes? Draw a picture of it. What do you think it would taste like?

Day Two: Adapt (F, T, C)
Task: Pizza is usually a casual meal that is commonly served at informal get togethers. Pretend that you have to create a pizza for a different type of gathering (a formal gathering, for instance) or for a different part of the meal (dessert, for instance). What would your new food be like? Maybe you would like to make it for your next meal.

Day Three: Put to a Different Use (F, T, C)
Task: How many different uses can you think of for a pizza cutter BESIDES cutting pizza?

Day Four: Risk-Taking (F)
Task: Pizza is a food that originated in Italy. Think of a type of international food that your family has never tried. Either go to a restaurant or prepare a dish at home from this international cuisine. How was it? Would you try this again? Why or why not?

Week Twenty Theme: Pizza

Day Five: Humor (F, T, C)

Task: What if the toppings on a pizza could talk to each other? What would they say? Prepare a humorous dialogue among them. For instance, maybe the pepper says, "Is it hot in here, or is it just me?"

Day Six: Curiosity (F, T, C)

Task: Brainstorm as many What If questions as you can think of about pizza. For example, what if pizza grew on trees? What if pizza was packaged in toothpaste tubes?

Day Seven: Drawing Prompt (F, T, C)

Task: Copy the drawing prompt below onto a piece of plain paper. Using the subject "thirty minutes or less," what can you draw while using the prompt as part of your picture? Can you include a background? What will you call your drawing?

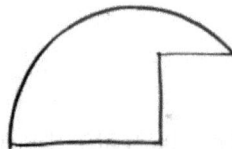

Week Twenty-One Theme: Things That Are Free

Day One: Elaborate (F, T, C)
Task: Imagine that you had the entire day free with no obligations, no chores, and no places to go. What would you do? Talk through the sequence of events for your free day, providing as much detail as you possibly can.

Day Two: Reflection (F, T, C)
Task: Do you think that all people should be free to do whatever they want with no rules or constraints? Why or why not? Are there certain people who should be able to? Or certain times of your life when you should be able to? Why or why not? What would the world be like if everyone was free to do whatever they want?

Day Three: Oxymorons (F, T, C)
Task: Oxymorons are phrases that combine two opposite words to convey a new idea. How do you explain some of these oxymorons related to "free?" Can you think of some examples where you might encounter these?

- Free speech
- Free gift
- Freedom is not free
- Free charge
- Free trade
- Free space

Day Four: Symbolism (F, T, C)
Task: If you had to choose one or more symbols to represent what it means to be free, which ones would you choose from the list below? What do these symbols represent to you? Can you create any additional symbols on your own?

- Bird
- Fist
- Lightbulb
- Brain
- Heart
- Compass
- Wind Blowing
- Waves
- Fire

Day Five: Museum Walk (F, T, C)
Task: Have each person create a poster about what freedoms matter most to them. You can create these on your own or cut them out of a magazine. Hang the posters around the room. Have each person rotate to each poster and write/draw responses to either:

- Add more detail
- Ask clarifying or challenging questions
- Agree or disagree

Day Six: Direct Analogy (F, T, C)
Task: How many similarities can you think of between a highway and the idea of freedom? How many differences can you think of?

Week Twenty-One Theme: Things That Are Free

Day Seven: A Puzzling Situation (F, T, C)

Task: Look at the picture below. What do you suppose is going on here? What details do you notice in the picture? What questions do you have? What do you think happened? What do you think will happen next?

Week Twenty-Two Theme: Things Associated With Water

Day One: Observation (F, T, C)
Task: Brainstorm a list of items that you can test out in water. Which ones float? Which ones sink? How do different items sound underwater? How does the view of something change after you put it underwater? Keep a journal of your observations.

Day Two: Internal Visualization (F, T, C)
Task: If you could live underwater (maybe in the ocean or in a pond), what do you think you would see? What would you do?

Day Three: Missing Information (F, T, C)
Task: Suppose that someone dressed very officially walked up to you and asked whether you would be going by air, land, or water. What information do you need to know in order to make the decision? How will you make the decision? What decision will you make?

Day Four: Aesthetic Thinking (F, T, C)
Task: Pretend that you are floating in the water. It could be in a boat, on a float, or on your back. It could be in the ocean, in the bathtub, or in a pool. What would you do? What would you see along the way? What would you hear on your journey? What smells might you encounter? What would it feel like?

Week Twenty-Two Theme: Things Associated With Water

Day Five: Negative Brainstorming (F, T, C)
Task: Brainstorm as many BAD examples as you can think of for water. It could be things that you wouldn't want to do WITH and/or IN water.

Day Six: Role-Playing (F, T, C)
Task: Create and act out a skit about a pirate or submarine. Who will play each role and what will they do? What will each person say? What costumes and props will you incorporate into your skit? What might go wrong during the countdown? How will you solve the problem?

Day Seven: Drawing Prompt (F, T, C)
Task: Copy the drawing prompt below onto a piece of plain paper. Using the subject "away we go," what can you draw while using the prompt as part of your picture? Can you include a background? What will you call your drawing?

Week Twenty-Three Theme: Animals

Day One: Figures of Speech (Metaphors and Analogies) (F, T, C)
Task: How would you complete or explain the figures of speech below that are related to animals? How many different responses can you brainstorm?

- An elephant is like ____.
- A wolf in sheep's clothing
- Animals are as amazing as ____.
- These classroom computers as old as ____.
- She is a workhorse.
- He is a chameleon.

Day Two: Social Activism (F, T, C)
Task: Select an organization that helps animals in some way. Some ideas include local animal shelters, the ASPCA, the World Wildlife Fund, etc. What can you do to help their cause? Can you volunteer somewhere? Collect needed items? Collect monetary donations? Put your care and concern into action!

Day Three: Rearrange (F, T, C)
Task: Select three animals that live in three different habitats. Now, rearrange these animals so that they must live in a different habitat from their own. If each animal was allowed three items to pack in a suitcase to help them survive in their new habitat, what should they each pack? What piece of advice would you give each animal to ensure their survival and happiness?

Week Twenty-Three Theme: Animals

Day Four: Flexibility (F, T, C)

Task: Choose a central area and place a large piece of paper there. Think of as many TYPES of animals as you can throughout the day. When you are done, try to brainstorm at least one example for each type you listed. How many types did you come up with?

Day Five: Problem Solving (F, T, C)

Task: The wildlife in your area is experiencing a lot of problems, because the city is taking over more and more of their habitat each day. What solutions can you brainstorm to help solve this? Can you come up with some creative solutions so that both the people and the animals are happy?

Week Twenty-Three Theme: Animals

Day Six: Internal Visualization (F, T, C)
Task: If you could go inside the brain of an animal of your choice for one day, what would your thoughts and feelings be about your life? What decisions would you make about what you do all day? Do you think you would prefer the animal life or the human life? Why?

Day Seven: A Puzzling Situation (F, T, C)
Task: Look at the picture below. What do you suppose is going on here? What details do you notice in the picture? What questions do you have? What do you think happened? What do you think will happen next?

Week Twenty-Four Theme: In the Classroom

Day One: Design Thinking (F, T, C)
Task: Think of a skill and/or subject matter that you think should be taught in school today but currently is not. What would it be? What would students need to know about it? How would it be taught? Who would teach it? What materials would you need? Design a classroom that teaches it.

Day Two: Personal Analogy (F, T, C)
Task: Pretend that you are a pencil in a classroom. Write a song, story, or poem in the first person about your experiences.

Day Three: Figures of Speech (Idioms) (F, T, C)
Task: School is frequently used in phrases to convey ideas. Some examples include:

- Hit the books
- Cut class
- Teach someone a lesson
- Pass with flying colors
- Learn the ropes
- Teacher's pet
- Bookworm
- Draw a blank

While these phrases are not meant to be literal, what if they were? Can you draw a picture or create a story using one of these figures of speech in a literal way?

Week Twenty-Four Theme: In the Classroom

Day Four: Aesthetic Thinking (F, T, C)
Task: Think about your life as a student. Now, think about the different subjects taught and the different areas of the school. What do you do in each one? What do you see along the way? What sounds do you hear? What new smells and tastes do you discover? What does each one feel like?

Day Five: Modify (F, T, C)
Task: How would school be different if the items below were suddenly MAGNIFIED (made much larger) or MINIMIZED (made much smaller)?

- Library
- Classrooms
- Cafeteria
- Playground
- Gym
- Length of the school day
- Length of various subjects
- School buses

Day Six: Change Management (F, T, C)
Task: Pretend that for one day, students and teachers had to switch roles. The one rule is that everyone would still have to carry out the responsibilities of their new roles. How would each group act? How would the things that need to be done at school get done? Do you think it would be a successful day? Why or why not? How might your answers be different if the people in charge (principal, assistant principal, etc.) had to switch roles with the teachers for a day? Do you think people's actions toward each other might change afterward? Why or why not?

Week Twenty-Four Theme:
In the Classroom

Day Seven: Drawing Prompt (F, T, C)

Task: Copy the drawing prompt below onto a piece of plain paper. Using the subject "raise your hand," what can you draw while using the prompt as part of your picture? Can you include a background? What will you call your drawing?

Week Twenty-Five Theme: Summer

Day One: Movement and Sound (F, T, C)
Task: Have a color song dance party! Think of as many songs as you can think of to listen and dance to that pertain to summer. Some ideas might include:

- "Summer Nights" by Olivia Newton John
- "Under the Boardwalk" by The Drifters
- "Summer in the City" by The Lovin' Spoonful
- "Steal My Sunshine" by Len
- "Hot Fun in the Summertime" by Sly and the Family Stone
- "Walking on Sunshine" by Katrina and the Waves
- "Good Vibrations" by The Beach Boys
- "Cruel Summer" by Bananarama
- "Dancing in the Street" by Martha and the Vandellas
- "The Boys of Summer" by Don Henley
- "Soak Up the Sun" by Sheryl Crow
- "Love Shack" by the B-52s
- "A Summer Song" by Chad & Jeremy

Day Two: Eliminate (F, T, C)
Task: If you could permanently eliminate one aspect of summer from the world, what would it be and why? What effect do you think this would have on the rest of the world?

Day Three: Originality (F, T, C)
Task: How many creative and unusual ways can you think of to keep cool during the summer aside from the ordinary ones? For example, you could invent an ice cream hat!

Week Twenty-Five Theme: Summer

Day Four: Making Decisions Using Criteria (F, T)
Task: There are many places you could go during summer vacation, but how will you decide? Each person is allowed one nomination to consider. How will you judge your nominees? What is most important to you? Is it distance? Is it the destination? Is it cost? Brainstorm 4-5 questions to consider when making your choice and make sure that you word your questions in a positive way. For example, if you do not like to travel far, your question might read, "Which is the closest?" If you are more concerned about spending money wisely, your question might read, "Which is the least expensive?" Rate each nomination for each of your questions using a smiley face (3 points) for "Definitely," a squiggly face (2 points) for "Sort Of," and a sad face (1 point) for "Not Really." Add up the points for each nominee to determine the winner. How will you decide a winner if there is a tie for first place?

Day Five: Observation (F, T, C)
Task: Brainstorm a list of ways in which people, animals, and plants act differently during the summer than they do during the rest of the year. Keep a journal of your observations.

Day Six: Abstract Thinking (F, T, C)
Task: Do you think that summer is most like a hammer, a saw, or sandpaper? Why?

Week Twenty-Five Theme: Summer

Day Seven: A Puzzling Situation (F, T, C)

Task: Look at the picture below. What do you suppose is going on here? What details do you notice in the picture? What questions do you have? What do you think happened? What do you think will happen next?

Week Twenty-Six Theme: Homes

Day One: Rearrange (F, T, C)
Task: Think about the layout of your present home. If you could rearrange things, what would your new home look like? Draw a new floorplan and explain the reasons for the changes.

Day Two: Emotions (F, T, C)
Task: Brainstorm a list of emotions that the idea of "home" brings about. What are the reasons for these emotions? Now, imagine that your family had to find a new place to call home. How would your emotions change?

Day Three: Social Activism (F, T, C)
Task: As a family, investigate ways in which people in your area who do not have a home need help. Some ideas might be lack of food, lack of shelter, lack of proper healthcare, lack of clothing, or lack of employment. What can you do to help? Put your care and concern into action!

Day Four: Design Thinking (F, T, C)
Task: If you could design the ultimate dream home for your family and money was no object, what would it include? Who would live in the house? What special features would bring each of these people happiness? Create a diagram or a 3D model of your new dream home.

Week Twenty-Six Theme: Homes

Day Five: Direct Analogy (F, T, C)

Task: In what ways are a human home and an animal home similar? In what ways are they different? Try to think of as many examples as possible.

Day Six: Collaboration (F)

Task: Think of a big home improvement project in your household that you could work on together. Collaborate together to get it done. First, come up with a plan to determine who will be responsible for which parts of the job to get the whole job done. Be prepared to adjust your plan if needed!

Day Seven: Drawing Prompt (F, T, C)

Task: Copy the drawing prompt below onto a piece of plain paper. Using the subject "no place like home," what can you draw while using the prompt as part of your picture? Can you include a background? What will you call your drawing?

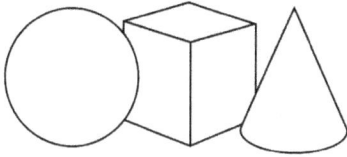

Week Twenty-Seven Theme: Shapes

Day One: Combine (F, T, C)
Task: Look at the shapes in the picture below. Can you combine them to create something new? What will it be?

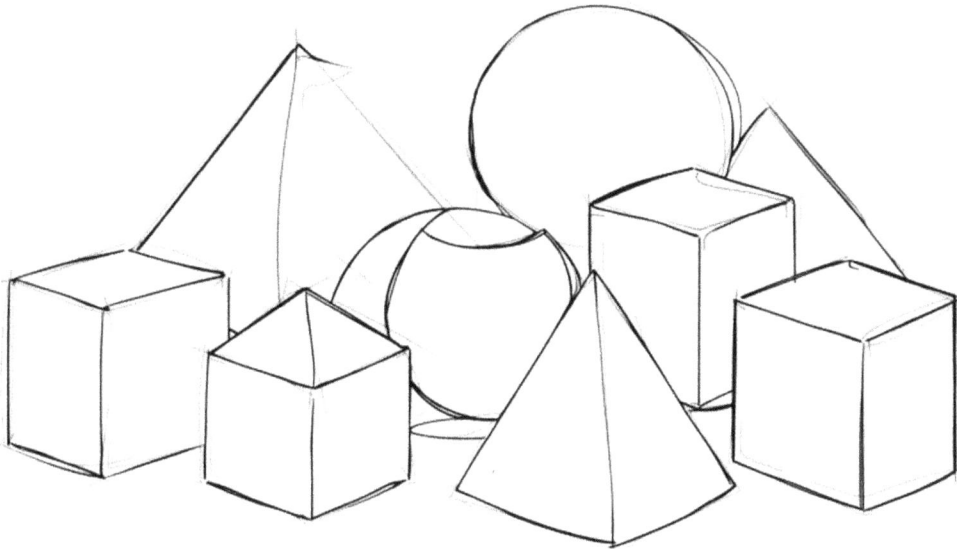

Day Two: Fluency (F, T, C)
Task: Choose a central area to place a large piece of paper and use it to record as many shapes as you can find today. Where did you see each one? Revisit the list as often as necessary throughout the day. How many did you brainstorm?

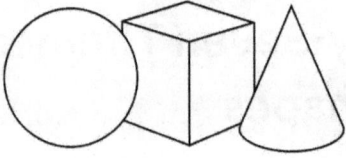

Week Twenty-Seven Theme: Shapes

Day Three: Design Thinking (F, T, C)
Task: Geometric shapes are used a lot in architecture. Can you design a pop-up town made entirely of geometric shapes? Don't forget to decorate your town! What will you include? What will you name your town?

Day Four: Observation (F, T, C)
Task: For the day, keep a journal or list of all of the shapes that you can find in nature. The hexagon in a honeycomb and the circles in tree rings are good examples. At the end of the day, compare lists. Cross off any words or ideas that are identical. Who thought of the most original ideas?

Day Five: Personal Analogy (F, T, C)
Task: Pretend that you are a triangle. Write a song, story, or poem in the first person about your experiences.

Day Six: Symbolism (F, T, C)
Task: If you had to choose a shape to represent each idea below, which ones would you choose and why?

- Love
- Fear
- Happiness
- Grief
- Freedom
- Knowledge
- Success
- Friendship
- Honesty

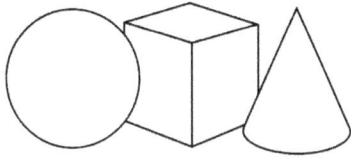

Week Twenty-Seven Theme: Shapes

Day Seven: A Puzzling Situation (F, T, C)

Task: Look at the picture below. What do you suppose is going on here? What details do you notice in the picture? What questions do you have? What do you think happened? What do you think will happen next?

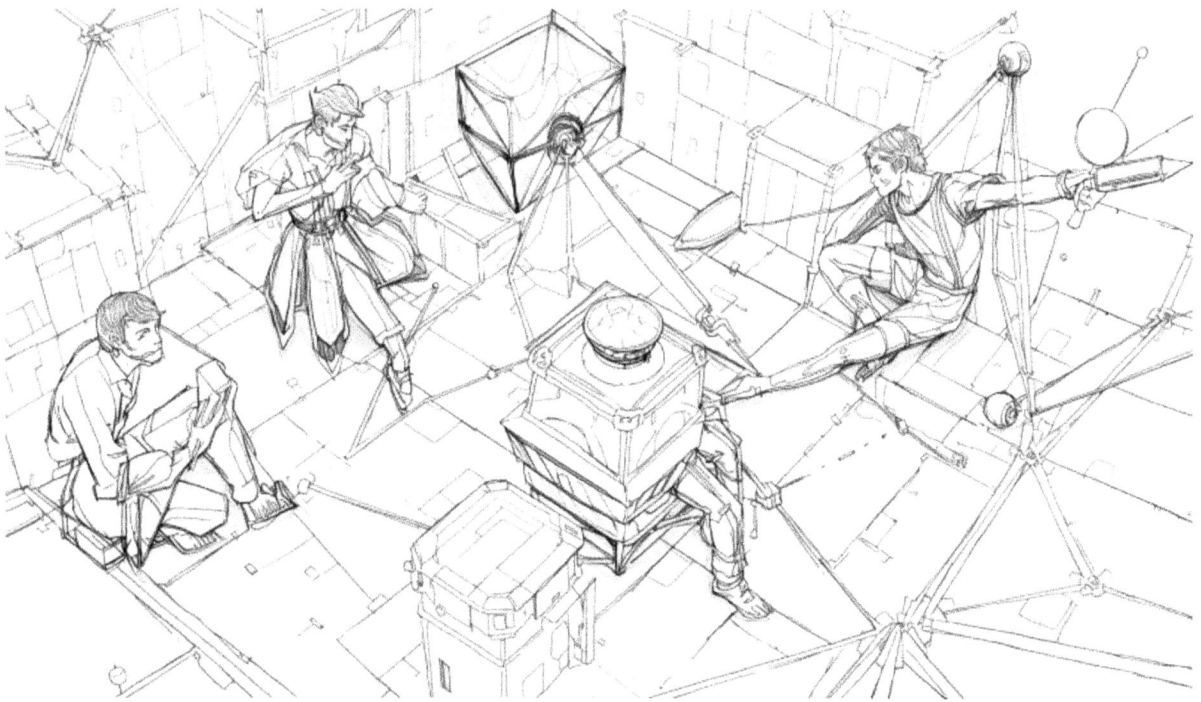

Week Twenty-Eight Theme: Growth

Day One: Internal Visualization (F, T, C)
Task: If you were a baby either inside of an egg or inside or a mother's belly, what do you think you would see? What would you do?

Day Two: Substitution (F, T, C)
Task: If you could choose an aspect of growing up to substitute with something else, what would it be? Some examples of aspects of growing up might be learning new things, learning social skills, body changes, peer pressure, gaining independence, taking on more responsibility, and solving problems.

Day Three: Figures of Speech (Metaphors and Analogies) (F, T, C)
Task: How would you complete or explain the figures of speech below that are related to growth? How many different responses can you brainstorm?

- A plant is like ____.
- "Don't go through life, grow through life." -Eric Butterworth
- Growth is as challenging as ____.
- Great oaks from little acorns grow.
- Plant the seeds.
- Reach for the stars.

Week Twenty-Eight Theme: Growth

Day Four: Curiosity (F, T, C)
Task: Brainstorm as many questions as you can think of about growth. Use some of the question stems below to help you. What answers can you come up with?

- Who? What? Where? When? Why? How?
- What if?
- Why is _____ important?
- How would things be different if?

Day Five: Emotions (F, T, C)
Task: How do you think your emotions change throughout your lifetime? How does the way you express these emotions change? Think about moving from being a baby to a toddler to a child to a teenager to a young adult to an adult and to an elderly person. What changes in regard to emotions and the expression of those emotions? How does this demonstrate personal growth?

Day Six: Brainstorming Solutions (F, T, C)
Task: Brainstorm possible solutions for each problem below that is commonly experienced as we grow up.

- Dealing with a bully
- Dealing with peer pressure
- Dealing with stress
- Changing schools and/or homes
- Making new friends

Week Twenty-Eight Theme: Growth

Day Seven: Drawing Prompt (F, T, C)

Task: Copy the drawing prompt below onto a piece of plain paper. Using the subject "growing on you," what can you draw while using the prompt as part of your picture? Can you include a background? What will you call your drawing?

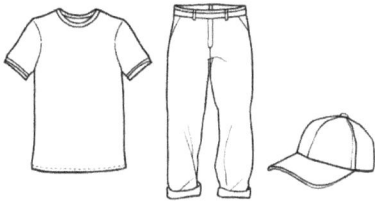

Week Twenty-Nine Theme: Clothes

Day One: Elaboration (F, T, C)

Task: Think of a special event that you have coming up. What is the most elaborate outfit that you can create for this occasion? Be sure to think of all of the details from the shoes to accessories to hairstyle to outfit.

Day Two: Making Judgments (F, T, C)

Task: Accepted "rules" about clothing have changed a lot over time. Looking at the statements below, do you agree or disagree with these? Why?

- In the 1800s, the clothes you wore revealed your place in society.
- In the 1900s, people began to move away from the norm.
- In the 2000s, people began to follow celebrity trends.
- Clothing can be a form of protest, conformity, or personal statement.

Day Three: Mind Map (F, T, C)

Task: Using a model similar to the one below, create a mind map about clothing. Write "clothing" in the center circle and then think of some "big ideas" related to clothing (outer wear, pajamas, etc.) to label the circles branching out from the center. You may use words and/or pictures to represent your ideas. Describe these big ideas further by connecting more circles and branches and labeling those with words and/or pictures. How detailed can you get?

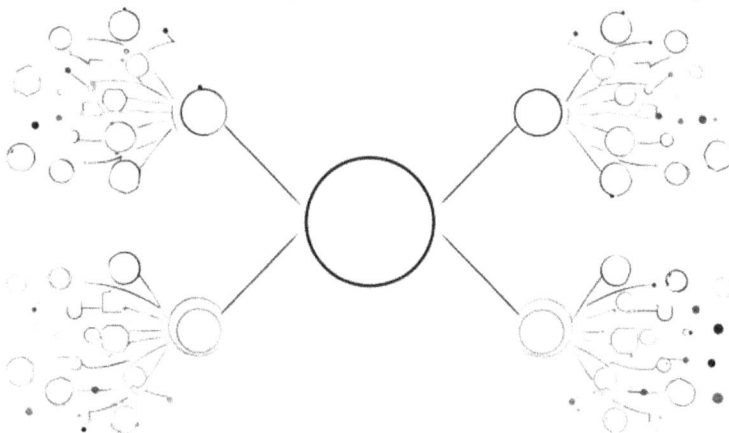

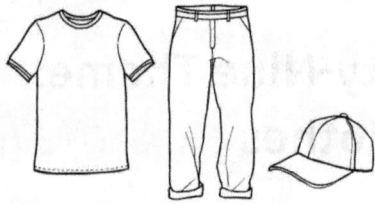

Week Twenty-Nine Theme: Clothes

Day Four: Solving Problems (F, T, C)
Task: Often, we encounter problems with our clothing that must be solved. How could solve some of these common daily annoyances?

- Improper fit
- Lack of pockets
- Stains
- Shrinking
- Wrinkles
- Tears and holes
- Lost buttons
- Discomfort

Day Five: Collaboration (F, C)
Task: As a family, reorganize your closets and dressers. First, come up with a plan to determine who will be responsible for which parts of the job to get the whole job done. Be prepared to adjust your plan if needed! Donate any items that you no longer want or need.

Day Six: Substitution (F, T, C)
Task: If you could substitute your shoes with other non-clothing items, what would it be like? What if you used watermelons? Or boxes? What else can you think of?

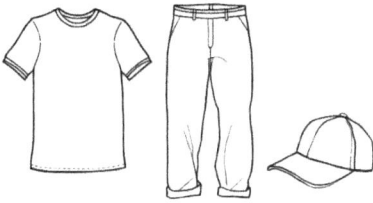

Week Twenty-Nine Theme: Clothes

Day Seven: A Puzzling Situation (F, T, C)

Task: Look at the picture below. What do you suppose is going on here? What details do you notice in the picture? What questions do you have? What do you think happened? What do you think will happen next?

Week Thirty Theme: In the Bathroom

Day One: Pros and Cons (F, T, C)
Task: Make a list of all of the pros and cons you can think of for taking a shower and for taking a bath? What similarities do you notice? Which do you prefer? Why?

Day Two: Adapt (F, T, C)
Task: Suppose that you needed to use your bathroom for a different purpose, such as doing the laundry, sleeping, or making dinner? Can you brainstorm ideas about how to get those tasks done?

Day Three: Challenging Norms (F, T, C)
Task: There are some things that are generally considered to be unwritten guidelines about how to act in a public bathroom. Do you agree with these? Why or why not?

- Flush the toilet after every use.
- Wipe up water that you splash out of the sink.
- Clean up your own messes.
- Don't talk on your cell phone.
- Mind your own business.
- Don't use the wheelchair accessible stall unless you need it.

Week Thirty Theme: In the Bathroom

Day Four: Humor (F, T, C)

Task: Can you use the prompts below to create "bathroom humor" jokes? How many different jokes can you make?

- What do you call a house with no bathroom?
- Why was the toilet sad?
- What did the sink say on the first day on the job?
- What does a hippopotamus keep in the medicine cabinet?
- What did the shower curtain say to the bathtub?
- Why did the cat enjoy looking in the bathroom mirror so much?

Day Five: Reflection (F, T, C)

Task: The bathroom is one place in the house where people may find some quiet time for reflection. What are your thoughts on these great mysteries of life?

- What is the meaning of life?
- Are we alone in the universe?
- Why do so many people disappear in the Bermuda Triangle?
- Why do bad things happen to good people?
- What happens to all of the socks that get lost in the dryer?

Day Six: Active Listening (F, T, C)

Task: What are some annoyances that you experience when you share a bathroom with someone else? Practice active listening by discussing this. The first person states their answer and a reason for it. The next person can choose to either agree or disagree respectfully by restating what the first person said and then stating their answer. Follow this format for the remainder of the discussion. How long can you keep the conversation going?

Week Thirty Theme:
In the Bathroom

Day Seven: Drawing Prompt (F, T, C)

Task: Copy the drawing prompt below onto a piece of plain paper. Using the subject "create your own oasis," what can you draw while using the prompt as part of your picture? Can you include a background? What will you call your drawing?

Week Thirty-One Theme: Sports

Day One: Curiosity (F, T, C)

Task: Brainstorm as many questions as you can think of about sports. Use some of the question stems below to help you. What answers can you come up with?

- Who? What? Where? When? Why? How?
- What if?
- Why is _____ important?
- How would things be different if?

Day Two: Experimentation (F, T, C)

Task: Gather several balls of different sizes and weights. Conduct some physics experiments with them, such as dropping different types of balls from a height, rolling two different types of balls toward each other to collide, or bouncing a ball with different amounts of force. What were your results? What adjustments can you make to your experiment to change your outcomes?

Day Three: Put to a Different Use (F, T, C)

Task: How many different uses can you come up with for a tennis racquet other than playing tennis?

Day Four: Flexibility (F, T, C)

Task: Choose a central area and place a large piece of paper there. Think of as many TYPES of sports as you can throughout the day. When you are done, try to brainstorm at least one example for each type you listed. How many types did you come up with?

Week Thirty-One Theme: Sports

Day Five: Pros and Cons (F, T, C)
Task: Make a list of all of the pros and cons you can think of for playing sports. How would your answers change depending upon the sport being played? What are some pros and cons for watching sports?

Day Six: Movement and Sound (F, T, C)
Task: Gather some random items from around you. Now, use them to create a new sporting game. What are the rules? What is the object of the game? What adjustments do you need to make as you play the game for the first time?

Day Seven: A Puzzling Situation (F, T, C)
Task: Look at the picture below. What do you suppose is going on here? What details do you notice in the picture? What questions do you have? What do you think happened? What do you think will happen next?

Week Thirty-Two Theme: Success

Day One: Museum Walk (F, T, C)
Task: Have each person create a poster about what it means to be successful. You can create these on your own or cut them out of a magazine. Hang the posters around the room. Have each person rotate to each poster and write/draw add new ideas (comments, more details, questions, etc.). Feel free to come back to the posters throughout the day to add additional items and words of encouragement.

Day Two: Eliminate (F, T, C)
Task: What obstacles do people have to overcome in order to be successful? If you could eliminate these obstacles, what do you think would happen? Do you think that success would be as meaningful if these obstacles were not in place? Why or why not?

Day Three: Abstract Thinking (F, T, C)
Task: Do you think that success is most like a banana, a chair, or a penny? Why?

Day Four: Perspectives (F, T, C)
Task: How do you think the idea of success changes depending on factors, such as your age or circumstances? How might each of the following groups define success?

- Family
- Community
- Classroom
- Workplace
- Friends
- Team

Week Thirty-Two Theme: Success

Day Five: Missing Information (F, T, C)
Task: Suppose that someone walked up to you and whispered, "Were you successful?" What information do you need to know in order to answer?

Day Six: Making Judgments (F, T, C)
Task: Looking at the statements below, do you think that they are true or false? Why?

- Success is the result of good judgment.
- Mistakes are part of success.
- Success is process of building up on previous successes.
- Success is your responsibility.
- Hard work is necessary for success.
- In order to be successful, you have to love your work.

Day Seven: Drawing Prompt (F, T, C)
Task: Copy the drawing prompt below onto a piece of plain paper. Using the subject "the secret to success," what can you draw while using the prompt as part of your picture? Can you include a background? What will you call your drawing?

Week Thirty-Three Theme: Fruits & Veggies

Day One: Humor (F, T, C)
Task: If fruits and veggies could talk to each other, what do you think they would say? Prepare a humorous dialogue among them. For example, maybe the orange says to the veggies, "Orange you glad we met?"

Day Two: Risk-taking (F)
Task: Go to the grocery store and explore the produce department. Find some fruits and veggies that you have never tried before and give them a try. How was it? Would you try this again? Why or why not?

Day Three: Brainstorming Solutions (F, T, C)
Task: We all know how important fruits and veggies are in our diets. Half of our plates should consist of them for every meal, but some people don't like them as much as others. What are some creative ways to get people who don't like them to eat them? Try to think of as many ways as you can.

Day Four: Elaboration (F, T, C)
Task: Pretend that you have to create a fruit tray and a veggie tray for a special occasion. What will you include? Will you have any dips? Will you cut them or arrange them in a special way? Be sure to elaborate and think of as many details as possible.

Week Thirty-Three Theme: Fruits & Veggies

Day Five: Active Listening (F, T, C)
Task: What are your favorite and least favorite fruits and veggies? Practice active listening by discussing this. The first person states their answer and a reason for it. The next person can choose to either agree or disagree respectfully by restating what the first person said and then stating their answer. Follow this format for the remainder of the discussion. How long can you keep the conversation going?

Day Six: Divergent and Convergent Thinking (F, T, C)
Task: Using small index cards or pieces of paper, brainstorm as many things as you can think of that are associated with fruits and veggies. Write each item on a separate card or piece of paper. After you have brainstormed as many as you can, how can you group these into categories? Which ones do you feel belong together? Why do they belong together? How many different ways can you come up with to group your words?

Week Thirty-Three Theme:
Fruits & Veggies

Day Seven: A Puzzling Situation (F, T, C)

Task: Look at the picture below. What do you suppose is going on here? What details do you notice in the picture? What questions do you have? What do you think happened? What do you think will happen next?

Week Thirty-Four Theme: Fall

Day One: Pros and Cons (F, T, C)
Task: Make a list of all of the pros and cons you can think of for fall. Try to think of all aspects from the weather to obligations to holidays to clothing-anything you can brainstorm!

Day Two: Fluency (F, T, C)
Task: Choose a central area to place a large piece of paper and use it to record as many phrases as you can think of that contain the word "fall." For example, you might list fall down or freefall. Revisit the list as often as necessary throughout the day. How many did you brainstorm together?

Day Three: Missing Information (F, T, C)
Task: Suppose that someone walked up to you and asked, "Did they fall for it?" What information do you need to know in order to answer?

Week Thirty-Four Theme: Fall

Day Four: Figures of Speech (Idioms) (F, T, C)
Task: Fall is frequently used in phrases to convey ideas. Some examples include:

- Fall in love
- Fall short
- Take the fall
- Fall into the wrong hands
- Fall behind
- The apple doesn't fall far from the tree.
- Fall into someone's lap
- Fall between the cracks

While these phrases are not meant to be literal, what if they were? Can you draw a picture or create a story using one of these figures of speech in a literal way?

Day Five: Aesthetic Thinking (F, T, C)
Task: Pretend that you are going for a long walk on a nice fall day. Where would you go? What would you do along the way? What would you see along the way? What would you hear on your journey? What smells might you encounter? What would it feel like?

Day Six: Adapt (F, T, C)
Task: Can you brainstorm ideas about how people, animals, and plants adapt for the season of fall? How do they deal with the changing weather? How do they deal with longer nights and shorter days? What preparations do they make before the arrival of winter?

Week Thirty-Four Theme: Fall

Day Seven: Drawing Prompt (F, T, C)
Task: Copy the drawing prompt below onto a piece of plain paper. Using the subject "fall into place," what can you draw while using the prompt as part of your picture? Can you include a background? What will you call your drawing?

Week Thirty-Five Theme: Feelings

Day One: Solving Problems (F, T, C)

Task: There are many problematic situations associated with feelings. How many solutions can you brainstorm to solve these common problems:

- A fight with a friend or family member
- Being lonely
- The stress of a special occasion
- Being sick or injured
- Problems at work or school

Day Two: Perspectives (F, T, C)

Task: Your feelings about a situation may be very different depending on your perspective. How might each perspective feel about each situation below?

- A game of baseball (winning team vs. losing team)
- A fight over a toy (an older sibling vs. a younger sibling)
- Cutting down trees to build an office building (a business person vs. someone who lives nearby)
- A struggle over cleaning a messy bedroom (child vs. parent)

How might it be helpful to look at the other person's perspective before reacting in a situation?

Week Thirty-Five Theme: Feelings

Day Three: Making Judgments (F, T, C)

Task: Looking at the statements below, do you think that they are true or false? Why?

- You should be happy at a wedding.
- You should be sad at a funeral.
- Men should not show their feelings as much as women do.
- Women should be nurturing and caring.
- Animals do not have feelings.

Day Four: Oxymorons (F, T, C)

Task: Oxymorons are phrases that combine two opposite words to convey a new idea. How do you explain some of these oxymorons related to feelings? Can you think of some examples where you might encounter these?

- Bittersweet
- Sweet sorrow
- Silent scream
- Happy tears
- Joyful despair
- Fiery ice
- Living death

Week Thirty-Five Theme: Feelings

Day Five: Yes, and... (F, T, C)

Task: Using the prompt "When ____ happens, I feel ____ because ____," take turns to complete the sentence. The next person should follow with "Yes, and...." in order to agree and add more details. Continue until everyone has contributed to the line of discussion. Then, someone else will take a turn to complete the prompt with a different type of situation and feeling, allowing others to follow with "Yes, and..." statements. How long can you keep the conversation going?

Day Six: Role-Playing (F, T, C)

Task: Create and act out a skit about an unexpected phone call that causes a mixture of feelings and reactions. Who will call? What will they say? Who will play each role and what will their jobs be? What will each person say? What costumes and props will you incorporate into your skit? What might go wrong? What will the outcome be?

Week Thirty-Five Theme: Feelings

Day Seven: A Puzzling Situation (F, T, C)

Task: Look at the picture below. What do you suppose is going on here? What details do you notice in the picture? What questions do you have? What do you think happened? What do you think will happen next?

Week Thirty-Six Theme:
In the Garden

Day One: Experimentation (F, T, C)

Task: Gather some plastic cups, dirt, water, and various seeds. Plant each of them and see how many you are able to grow. Once they are growing, experiment with different variables, such as exposure to different amounts of light, different temperatures, or different types of music. What were your results? What adjustments can you make to your experiment to change your outcomes?

Day Two: Fantasy (F, T, C)

Task: Pretend that you could grow things in a garden that do not typically grow in a garden. For example, you could grow school supplies or electronics. What would you grow? How would you ensure a good crop? What would your garden need to grow? How would you harvest and when? How would you transport your goods and where would you sell them? What do you think would happen?

Day Three: Direct Analogy (F, T, C)

Task: In what ways are a garden and a computer similar? In what ways are they different? Try to think of as many examples as possible.

Week Thirty-Six Theme: In the Garden

Day Four: Figures of Speech (Idioms) (F, T, C)
Task: Things associated with gardens are frequently used in phrases to convey ideas. Some examples include:

- Nip it in the bud
- Barking up the wrong tree
- Have a green thumb
- Garden variety
- Grow like a weed
- Late bloomer
- A bed of roses

While these phrases are not meant to be literal, what if they were? Can you draw a picture or create a story using one of these figures of speech in a literal way?

Day Five: Personal Analogy (F, T, C)
Task: Pretend that you are a seed. Write a song, story, or poem in the first person about your experiences.

Day Six: Rearrange (F, T, C)
Task: Think about how different things in a garden grow (on a tree, underground, underwater, on a vine, on a bush, etc.). If you could rearrange things, what would your new garden look like? Draw your new garden.

Week Thirty-Six Theme:
In the Garden

Day Seven: Drawing Prompt (F, T, C)
Task: Copy the drawing prompt below onto a piece of plain paper. Using the subject "garden variety," what can you draw while using the prompt as part of your picture? Can you include a background? What will you call your drawing?

Week Thirty-Seven Theme: Books

Day One: Fantasy (F, T, C)
Task: Read a fantasy book that has been made into a movie. Then watch the movie. How were the book and the movie the same? How were they different? What questions would you ask the author and the director if you could? How would you have made the book and/or the movie differently?

Day Two: Curiosity (F, T, C)
Task: Brainstorm as many questions as you can think of about the books that you have read. Use some of the question stems below to help you. What answers can you come up with?

- Who? What? Where? When? Why? How?
- What if?
- Why is _____ important?
- How would things be different if?

Day Three: Role-Playing (F, T, C)
Task: Act out a book that has NOT been made into a movie or play. Who will play each role and what will their jobs be? What will each person say? What costumes and props will you incorporate into your skit? Invite some family and/or friends over to watch your production!

Week Thirty-Seven Theme: Books

Day Four: Combining (F, T, C)

Task: Can you combine the main characters from two different books together to create something new? How would it work? What would be the main plot of the new book? What would happen in the book?

Day Five: Put to a Different Use (F, T, C)

Task: How many different uses can you think of for a book other than reading?

Day Six: Social Activism (F, T, C)

Task: Reading books helps us improve our memories, focus, and expand our vocabulary and knowledge. Decide how you can promote reading. Some ideas include donating books to an organization, creating a lending library for your neighborhood, or simply visiting your local public library. Put your care and concern into action!

Week Thirty-Seven Theme: Books

Day Seven: A Puzzling Situation (F, T, C)
Task: Look at the picture below. What do you suppose is going on here? What details do you notice in the picture? What questions do you have? What do you think happened? What do you think will happen next?

Week Thirty-Eight Theme: On the Farm

Day One: Divergent and Convergent Thinking (F, T, C)
Task: Using small index cards or pieces of paper, brainstorm as many things as you can think of that you might see on a farm. Write each item on a separate card or piece of paper. After you have brainstormed as many as you can, how can you group these into categories? Which ones do you feel belong together? Why do they belong together? How many different ways can you come up with to group your words?

Day Two: Modify (F, T, C)
Task: How would farms be different if the tools that the farmers use to do their jobs were suddenly MAGNIFIED (made much larger) or MINIMIZED (made much smaller)?

- Shovel
- Hoe
- Tractor
- Plow
- Rake
- Wagon
- Wheelbarrow

Day Three: Symbolism (F, T, C)
Task: If you had to create emojis for texting that represent things on a farm, what would you create? Try to draw as many as you can.

Week Thirty-Eight Theme: On the Farm

Day Four: Originality (F, T, C)

Task: One problem that farmers encounter frequently is extreme weather. Choose one type of weather below and create a new way that does not already exist for farmers to protect their farms and crops during that type of weather. Create a diagram of your idea.

- Floods
- Droughts
- Frost
- Extreme heat
- Tornadoes

Day Five: Lateral Thinking (F, T, C)

Task: Pretend that you live on a farm. One day, you wake up and find all of the animals gone. What do you think might be going on? Why do you think that?

Day Six: Humor (F, T, C)

Task: What if farm animals could talk to each other? What would they say? Prepare a humorous dialogue among them. For instance, maybe the cow says, "How dairy you!"

Week Thirty-Eight Theme: On the Farm

Day Seven: Drawing Prompt (F, T, C)

Task: Copy the drawing prompt below onto a piece of plain paper. Using the subject "funny farm," what can you draw while using the prompt as part of your picture? Can you include a background? What will you call your drawing?

Week Thirty-Nine Theme: Holidays

Day One: Mind Map (F, T, C)

Task: Using a model similar to the one below, create a mind map about holidays. Write the word "holidays" in the center circle and then think of some "big ideas" related to holidays to label the circles branching out from the center. You may use words and/or pictures to represent your ideas. Describe these big ideas further by connecting more circles and branches and labeling those with words and/or pictures. How detailed can you get?

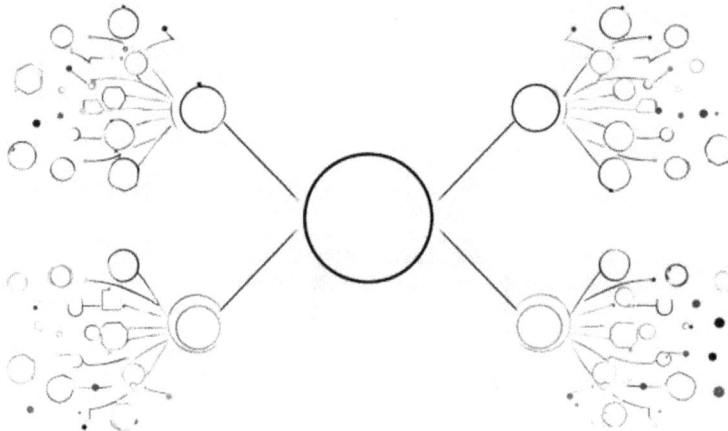

Day Two: Movement and Sound (F, T, C)

Task: Have a holiday song dance party! Think of as many songs as you can think of to listen and dance to. Some ideas might include:

- "All I Want for Christmas is You" by Mariah Carey
- "Jingle Bell Rock" by Bobby Helms
- "Rockin' Around the Christmas Tree" by Brenda Lee
- "Hanukkah, Oh Hanukkah"
- "The Chanukah Song" by Adam Sandler
- "8 Days of Hanukkah" by Sharon Jones & Dap-Kings
- "Born in the USA" by Bruce Springsteen
- "American Pie" by Don McLean

Week Thirty-Nine Theme: Holidays

Day Three: Collaboration (F, C)

Task: As a family, think of someone who may be having a hard time currently. Brainstorm ideas about how you can bring some holiday cheer to that person. You may even want to collaborate with other families to help you.

Day Four: Originality (F, T, C)

Task: If you could create a brand new holiday, what would it be? How would you celebrate? Would you serve special foods? Would you participate in special activities or traditions? What would you name your holiday?

Day Five: Substitution (F, T, C)

Task: Holidays are a time for tradition, but what would happen if you substituted some items for other things? For example, what if for Christmas, you decorated a telephone pole instead of a tree? Think of one or more substitutes for the traditional items below. How wild and crazy can you get?

- Exchanging gifts
- Hanging stockings over the fireplace
- Watching fireworks
- Making resolutions
- Lighting the menorah
- Playing dreidel
- Watching the parade
- Carving pumpkins
- Wearing a costume

Week Thirty-Nine Theme: Holidays

Day Six: Challenging Norms (F, T, C)

Task: There are some things that are generally considered to be unwritten guidelines about holidays. If you could challenge or change one or more of the holiday norms below, what would it be? Why?

- Always bring a gift for the party host.
- If you are hosting a party, you need to provide food and drink.
- Make sure to socialize with everyone at a party.
- There should be one table for adults and a separate one for children.
- People should have assigned seats at the table.
- You should dress up for holiday celebrations.
- Holiday decorating should not be done too early and should not stay up long after the holiday.

Day Seven: A Puzzling Situation (F, T, C)

Task: Look at the picture below. What do you suppose is going on here? What details do you notice in the picture? What questions do you have? What do you think happened? What do you think will happen next?

©CortIPimes.com

116

Week Forty Theme:
Ideas

Day One: Oxymorons (F, T, C)
Task: Oxymorons are phrases that combine two opposite words to convey a new idea. How do you explain some of these oxymorons related to ideas? Can you think of some examples where you might encounter these?

- Clearly misunderstood
- Falsely true
- Impossible solution
- Loyal opposition
- Open secret
- Random order
- Static flow
- Terribly good
- Unbiased opinion
- Wise fool

Day Two: Fluency (F, T, C)
Task: Choose a central area to place a large piece of paper and use it to record as many examples of great brand-new ideas as you can think of. For example, a plate that is self-cleaning would be a great time and energy saver. Revisit the list as often as necessary throughout the day. How many did you brainstorm together?

Week Forty Theme: Ideas

Day Three: Aesthetic Thinking (F, T, C)
Task: There are a lot of studies that show that certain smells, such as peppermint, or certain sounds, such as classical music, can help people think better. What types of sights, sounds, smells, tastes, and textures help you come up with the best ideas? How can you incorporate these into your workspace?

Day Four: Negative Brainstorming (F, T, C)
Task: Brainstorm as many BAD examples as you can think of for ideas. These can be real or imaginary. For instance, running a track meet while wearing ice skates would be a BAD idea.

Day Five: Risk-taking (F, T, C)
Task: Take the time today to try out an idea that you've thought of but were reluctant to try. Maybe it's a new hobby, activity, or skill.   Was it worth the risk? Would you try this again? Why or why not?

Day Six: Figures of Speech (Metaphors and Analogies) (F, T, C)
Task: How would you complete or explain the figures of speech below that are related to ideas? How many different responses can you brainstorm?

- A new idea is a seed.
- Seeing the light
- Laying the foundation
- As thoughtful as ____
- An idea is like ____
- Her brain was working like ____
- The idea was as good as ____

Week Forty Theme:
Ideas

Day Seven: Drawing Prompt (F, T, C)

Task: Copy the drawing prompt below onto a piece of plain paper. Using the subject "the spark of a great idea," what can you draw while using the prompt as part of your picture? Can you include a background? What will you call your drawing?

Week Forty-One Theme: Jungle

Day One: Direct Analogy (F, T, C)
Task: In what ways are a jungle and a couch similar? In what ways are they different? Try to think of as many examples as possible.

Day Two: Role-Playing (F, T, C)
Task: Create and act out a skit about a jungle expedition. Who will play each role and what will their jobs be? What will each person say? What costumes and props will you incorporate into your skit? What might go wrong during the expedition? How will you solve the problem?

Day Three: Reflection (F, T, C)
Task: It is said that it's a jungle out there. Do you think this is true? Why or why not? What can you do to help keep your "jungle" tamer?

Day Four: Modify (F, T, C)
Task: How would the jungle be different if the items below were suddenly MAGNIFIED (made much larger) or MINIMIZED (made much smaller)?

- Plants
- Mammals
- Reptiles
- Insects
- Rivers
- Weather

Week Forty-One Theme: Jungle

Day Five: Perspectives (F, T, C)

Task: Even though many living things may share the same space, their life experiences would be very different depending on their perspective. How might each perspective below experience life in a tree in the jungle?

- Monkey
- Parrot
- Tree frog
- Ant
- Python
- Sloth
- Butterfly

Day Six: Change Management (F, T, C)

Task: It is said that a lion is king of the jungle. Pretend that roles were switched and a different animal was now in charge. How would animals act differently? How would the food web be affected? Do you think it would be a successful jungle? Why or why not? Do you think people's actions toward the jungle might change afterward? Why or why not?

Week Forty-One Theme: Jungle

Day Seven: A Puzzling Situation (F, T, C)

Task: Look at the picture below. What do you suppose is going on here? What details do you notice in the picture? What questions do you have? What do you think happened? What do you think will happen next?

Week Forty-Two Theme:
In the Kitchen

Day One: Experimentation (F, T)
Task: Perform some kitchen science experiments. You can find some interesting possibilities online by searching "experiments in the kitchen for kids." You may even create some on your own! Some ideas include:

- Rock candy
- Cornstarch slime
- Fireworks in a jar
- Baking soda and vinegar volcano
- Ice cream in a bag
- Invisible ink
- Elephant toothpaste
- Floating eggs

Day Two: Flexibility (F, T, C)
Task: Choose a central area and place a large piece of paper there. Think of as many TYPES of kitchen items as you can throughout the day. When you are done, try to brainstorm at least one example for each type you listed. How many types did you come up with?

Day Three: Aesthetic Thinking (F, T, C)
Task: A kitchen is usually one of the busiest rooms in a home. Take some time to reflect on what goes on in your kitchen.   What do you see throughout the day? What would you hear? What do you smell and taste? What does it feel like?

Week Forty-Two Theme: In the Kitchen

Day Four: Yes, and... (F, T, C)
Task: Using the prompt "My favorite meal is ____, because ____," take turns to complete the sentence. The next person should follow with "Yes, and...." in order to agree and add more details. Continue until everyone has contributed to the line of discussion. Then, someone else will take a turn to complete the prompt with a different type of meal, allowing others to follow with "Yes, and..." statements. How long can you keep the conversation going?

Day Five: Put to a Different Use (F, T, C)
Task: How many different uses can you think of for a spatula BESIDES cooking?

Day Six: Lateral Thinking (F, T, C)
Task: One day, you wake up, go into the kitchen, and find that all of your utensils have disappeared overnight. What do you think might be going on? Why do you think that?

Week Forty-Two Theme: In the Kitchen

Day Seven: Drawing Prompt (F, T, C)

Task: Copy the drawing prompt below onto a piece of plain paper. Using the subject "what's cooking," what can you draw while using the prompt as part of your picture? Can you include a background? What will you call your drawing?

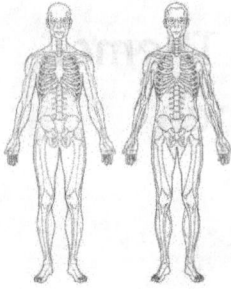

Week Forty-Three Theme: Body

Day One: Humor (F, T, C)
Task: What if your body parts could talk to each other? What would they say? Prepare a humorous dialogue among them. For instance, maybe after stubbing your big toe, your foot says, "Better call a toe truck!"

Day Two: Rearrange (F, T, C)
Task: What if you could rearrange your body parts for a specific purpose? Maybe you want to be taller, shorter, faster, etc. What would your new body look like? Draw your new body and explain the reasons for the changes.

Day Three: Fluency (F, T, C)
Task: Choose a central area to place a large piece of paper and use it to record as many ways to use your body parts to get from here to there as you can think of. Revisit the list as often as necessary throughout the day. How many did you brainstorm together? Was it more or less than the last time you brainstormed a list like this?

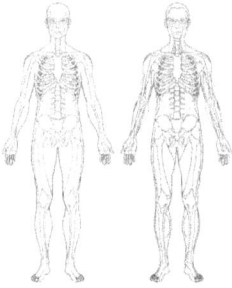

Week Forty-Three Theme: Body

Day Four: Figures of Speech (Metaphors and Analogies) (F, T, C)
Task: How would you complete or explain the figures of speech below that are related to the body? How many different responses can you brainstorm?

- A body is like ____.
- Finger is to hand as ____ is to ____.
- A body is as complicated as ____.
- Hat is to head as ____ is to ____.
- Mouth is to eat as ____ is to ____.
- Face up to the facts
- Keep you on your toes
- Rule of thumb
- Tongue-lashing

Day Five: Collaboration (F, T, C)
Task: Create an indoor or outdoor obstacle course that will use as many body parts as possible. Collaborate together to build it. Race your way through the obstacle course. Invite your neighbors and friends. Adjust the course as necessary for different age groups and ability levels.

Day Six: Movement and Sound (F, T, C)
Task: Brainstorm as many ways as you can think of to make SOUND by MOVING your body parts. Who is the champion?

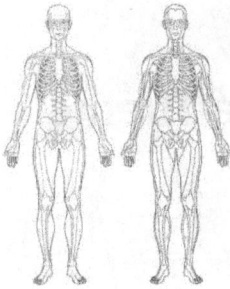

Week Forty-Three Theme: Body

Day Seven: A Puzzling Situation (F, T, C)

Task: Look at the picture below. What do you suppose is going on here? What details do you notice in the picture? What questions do you have? What do you think happened? What do you think will happen next?

Week Forty-Four Theme: Mountain

Day One: Figures of Speech (Idioms) (F, T, C)
Task: Mountains are frequently used in phrases to convey ideas. Some examples include:

- Move mountains
- Climb every mountain
- A mountain of money/responsibility
- Make a mountain out of a molehill
- Peak of success
- Mountain view

While these phrases are not meant to be literal, what if they were? Can you draw a picture or create a story using one of these figures of speech in a literal way?

Day Two: Negative Brainstorming (F, T, C)
Task: Brainstorm as many examples as you can think of that you CAN'T do on a mountain. Roller skating might be a good example.

Week Forty-Four Theme: Mountain

Day Three: Eliminate (F, T, C)
Task: If you could permanently eliminate each item listed below from a mountain, what effect do you think this would have? Do you think each should be eliminated? Why or why not?

- Peak
- Valley
- Trees
- Animals
- Hiking trails
- Snow
- Thin air
- Avalanches

Day Four: Pros and Cons (F, T, C)
Task: Make a list of all of the pros and cons you can think of for living on a mountain. How would your answers change depending upon whether you were an adult or a child? What are some pros and cons for NOT living on a mountain?

Day Five: Combining (F, T, C)
Task: Can you combine a mountain with something completely unrelated to create something new? What would the world be like if this really existed? For example, what if mountains were combined with ice cream?

Week Forty-Four Theme: Mountain

Day Six: Internal Visualization (F, T, C)
Task: If you could go inside a mountain, what do you think you would see? What would you do?

Day Seven: Drawing Prompt (F, T, C)
Task: Copy the drawing prompt below onto a piece of plain paper. Using the subject "the hardest climb," what can you draw while using the prompt as part of your picture? Can you include a background? What will you call your drawing?

Week Forty-Five Theme: Winter

Day One: Emotions (F, T, C)
Task: Many people suffer from Seasonal Affective Disorder during the wintertime. Brainstorm as many ways as you can think of to improve your mood if you begin to feel a little sad during winter.

Day Two: Museum Walk (F, T, C)
Task: Have each person create a poster about their favorite wintertime activities. You can create these on your own or cut them out of a magazine. Hang the posters around the room. Have each person rotate to each poster and write/draw questions, additional details, or comments. Feel free to come back to the posters throughout the day to add comments for each person.

Day Three: Abstract Thinking (F, T, C)
Task: Do you think that winter is most like a pillow, a can, or a football? Why?

Day Four: Substitution (F, T, C)
Task: What could you substitute snow with to make winter even better? What effect would this change have on the world?

Week Forty-Five Theme: Winter

Day Five: Experimentation (F, T, C)
Task: Experiment with different ways that you can think of to keep warm during the winter. Which ways work the best? Use your imagination!

Day Six: Elaboration (F, T, C)
Task: How can you decorate the snowman below as elaborately as possible? Try to think of as many details as possible.

Week Forty-Five Theme: Winter

Day Seven: A Puzzling Situation (F, T, C)
Task: Look at the picture below. What do you suppose is going on here? What details do you notice in the picture? What questions do you have? What do you think happened? What do you think will happen next?

Week Forty-Six Theme:
In the Country

Day One: Perspectives (F, T, C)
Task: Think about people who live in different countries around the world. What do you think each person would be most proud of in regard to their country? What do you think they like about living in their country? How do you think each would feel about visiting another country? How do your answers differ among different countries?

Day Two: Brainstorming Solutions (F, T, C)
Task: Pretend that you take a nice drive out in the country for the day. Your car breaks down, and you are not able to fix it. You also have no cell phone service. What will you do? How will you get back home?

Day Three: Making Decisions Using Criteria (F, T)
Task: There are many different countries that you could visit, but how will you decide if you had the chance? Each person is allowed one nomination to consider. How will you judge your nominees? What is most important to you? Is it fun? Is it distance? Is it cost? Brainstorm 4-5 questions to consider when making your choice and make sure that you word your questions in a positive way. For example, if you like fun, your question might read, "Which is the most fun?" If you are more concerned about spending money wisely, your question might read, "Which is the least expensive?" Rate each nomination for each of your questions using a smiley face (3 points) for "Definitely," a squiggly face (2 points) for "Sort Of," and a sad face (1 point) for "Not Really." Add up the points for each nominee to determine the winner. How will you decide a winner if there is a tie for first place?

Week Forty-Six Theme: In the Country

Day Four: Adapt (F, T, C)
Task: Suppose that a person who has only lived in the city decided to move to the country. What would they need to do in order to adapt to their new home? How about if a person who has only lived in the country decided to move to the city?

Day Five: Curiosity (F, T, C)
Task: Brainstorm as many questions as you can think of about other countries.

Day Six: Risk-taking (F)
Task: Try a new activity together that is associated with being in the country. Some ideas include hiking, wildlife photography, going on a picnic, playing outdoor games, birdwatching, or picking fruit. Was it worth the risk? Would you try this again? Why or why not?

Week Forty-Six Theme:
In the Country

Day Seven: Drawing Prompt (F, T, C)

Task: Copy the drawing prompt below onto a piece of plain paper. Using the subject "middle of nowhere," what can you draw while using the prompt as part of your picture? Can you include a background? What will you call your drawing?

Week Forty-Seven Theme: Pets

Day One: Solving Problems (F, T, C)
Task: How many ways can you come up with for this hamster to get away from this cat?

Day Two: Pros and Cons (F, T, C)
Task: Make a list of all of the pros and cons you can think of for having a pet. How would your answers change depending upon the type of pet you have? What are some pros and cons for NOT having a pet?

Week Forty-Seven Theme: Pets

Day Three: Missing Information (F, T, C)
Task: Suppose that a friend asks if you would please adopt his pet, because he was no longer able to care for it. What information do you need to know in order to answer?

Day Four: Change Management (F, T, C)
Task: Pretend that roles were switched at home and the pets had to take care of the humans instead. How would the pets act differently? How would the humans act differently? Do you think it would be successful? Why or why not? Do you think that this could be a permanent switch? Why or why not?

Day Five: Personal Analogy (F, T, C)
Task: Pretend that you are a pet goldfish in a bowl. Write a song, story, or poem in the first person about your experiences.

Day Six: Originality (F, T, C)
Task: If you could create the ideal pet that does not already exist, what would it be? What would it look like? Sound like? Act like? What would you name your pet? Be as detailed as possible.

Week Forty-Seven Theme: Pets

Day Seven: A Puzzling Situation (F, T, C)
Task: Look at the picture below. What do you suppose is going on here? What details do you notice in the picture? What questions do you have? What do you think happened? What do you think will happen next?

Week Forty-Eight Theme: Movies

Day One: Mind Map (F, T, C)

Task: Using a model similar to the one below, create a mind map about movies. Write the word "movies" in the center circle and then think of some "big ideas" related to movies to label the circles branching out from the center. You may use words and/or pictures to represent your ideas. Describe these big ideas further by connecting more circles and branches and labeling those with words and/or pictures. How detailed can you get?

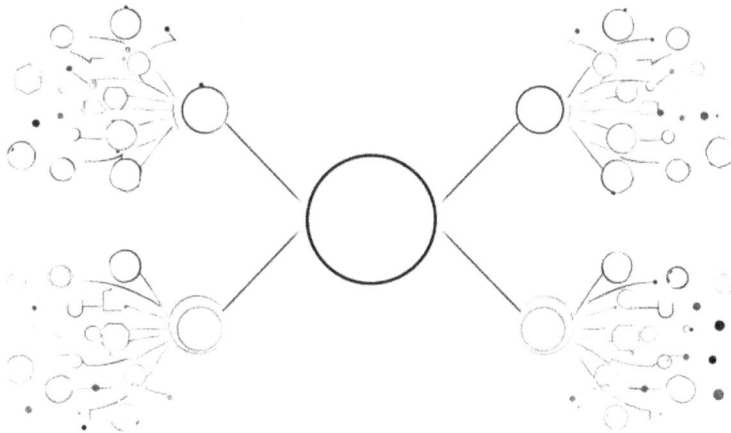

Day Two: Role-Playing (F, T, C)

Task: Play a game of charades by acting out movie scenes for others to guess. Who is the champion?

Day Three: Modify (F, T, C)

Task: Have you ever been unhappy about how a movie ended? How can you modify the ending to make it just perfect?

Week Forty-Eight Theme: Movies

Day Four: Challenging Norms (F, T, C)

Tasks: Norms are simply the way that we usually do things. If you could challenge or change one or more of the norms below associated with movies, what would it be? Why?

- That movie is so good, everyone should see it.
- Movies should be inspiring and thought-provoking.
- People should not talk during movies.
- People should not be on their cell phones during movies.
- The best seats in the movies theater are in the top back row center.

Day Five: Figures of Speech (Idioms) (F, T, C)

Task: Movies are frequently used in phrases to convey ideas. Some examples include:

- Blockbuster
- That's a wrap
- Cut to the chase
- Steal the show
- In the limelight
- A showstopper

While these phrases are not meant to be literal, what if they were? Can you draw a picture or create a story using one of these figures of speech in a literal way?

Day Six: Internal Visualization (F, T, C)

Task: If you could live your life inside of a movie, what would it be like? Which movie would you choose? Why?

Week Forty-Eight Theme: Movies

Day Seven: Drawing Prompt (F, T, C)

Task: Copy the drawing prompt below onto a piece of plain paper. Using the subject "lights, camera, action," what can you draw while using the prompt as part of your picture? Can you include a background? What will you call your drawing?

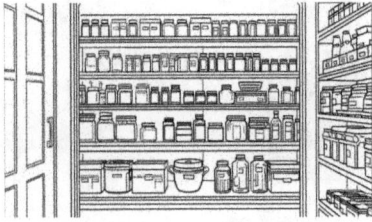

Week Forty-Nine Theme: In the Pantry

Day One: Social Activism (F)
Task: As a family, clean out your pantry. Are there any items that are still good, but you might not need? Collect and donate those items to a local food pantry or homeless shelter. Perhaps you could even make a trip to the grocery store to purchase additional items that are most in need. Put your care and concern into action!

Day Two: Combining (F, C)
Task: Look in your pantry for some items that look appetizing to you. Can you combine these to create a new snack? What will you name your new snack? Do you think others would buy this if it were for sale in stores? Why or why not?

Day Three: Put to a Different Use (F, T, C)
Task: How many different uses can you think of for an empty potato chip bag?

Day Four: Negative Brainstorming (F, T, C)
Task: Brainstorm as many BAD examples as you can think of for items that do NOT belong in a pantry. Some possible answers include ants and a symphony orchestra.

Day Five: Substitution (F, C)
Task: Take a look at the items in your pantry. Not all of them may be healthy choices. Can you think of some healthy substitutions that you can make for items that may not be considered healthy? Would you be willing to give these a try the next time that you go shopping? Why or why not?

Week Forty-Nine Theme: In the Pantry

Day Six: Problem Solving (F, T, C)
Task: Food insecurity is a big problem today. Some families cannot afford to purchase enough food to eat. If your family was experiencing this, what are some things that you could do to get the food that you need? Try to brainstorm as many solutions as possible.

Day Seven: A Puzzling Situation (F, T, C)
Task: Look at the picture below. What do you suppose is going on here? What details do you notice in the picture? What questions do you have? What do you think happened? What do you think will happen next?

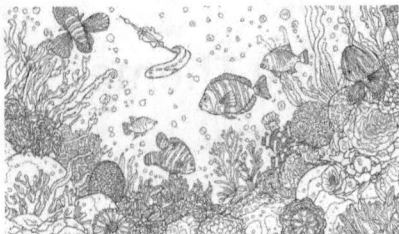

Week Fifty Theme: Ocean

Day One: Humor (F, T, C)
Task: What if the things found in the ocean could talk to each other? What would they say? Prepare a humorous dialogue among them. For instance, maybe the starfish says, "Look at me, everyone! I'm famous! I'm a star!"

Day Two: Divergent and Convergent Thinking (F, T, C)
Task: Using small index cards or pieces of paper, brainstorm as many things as you can think of that you might see in an ocean. It could be anything, not just animals! Write each item on a separate card or piece of paper. After you have brainstormed as many as you can, how can you group these into categories? Which ones do you feel belong together? Why do they belong together? How many different ways can you come up with to group your words?

Day Three: Modify (F, T, C)
Task: How would the world be different if the items below that are found in an ocean were suddenly MAGNIFIED (made much larger) or MINIMIZED (made much smaller)?

- Whales
- Sharks
- Sea snakes
- Kelp
- Sea turtles
- Jellyfish
- Octopus
- Coral reefs
- Shipwrecks
- Submarines
- Boats

Week Fifty Theme:
Ocean

Day Four: Symbolism (F, T, C)

Task: If you had to choose the symbolism for different ocean animals to represent, what would each one below mean? For example, maybe a starfish could be a symbol for something famous or outstanding. What would each one below represent to you?

- Dolphin
- Crab
- Penguin
- Pelican
- Polar bear
- Manatee
- Clownfish
- Sailfish
- Oyster

Day Five: Oxymorons (F, T, C)

Task: Oxymorons are phrases that combine two opposite words to convey a new idea. How do you explain some of these oxymorons related to oceans? Can you think of some examples where you might encounter these?

- Deafening silence
- Lifeless ocean
- Sunless sea
- Surrounded by water, but not a drop to drink
- Dependable unpredictability
- Living ocean
- Ecotourism

Week Fifty Theme: Ocean

Day Six: Adapt (F, T, C)

Task: Suppose that the fish below decided to move to the forest. What would it need in order to adapt to its new home? How would it be able to meet its needs?

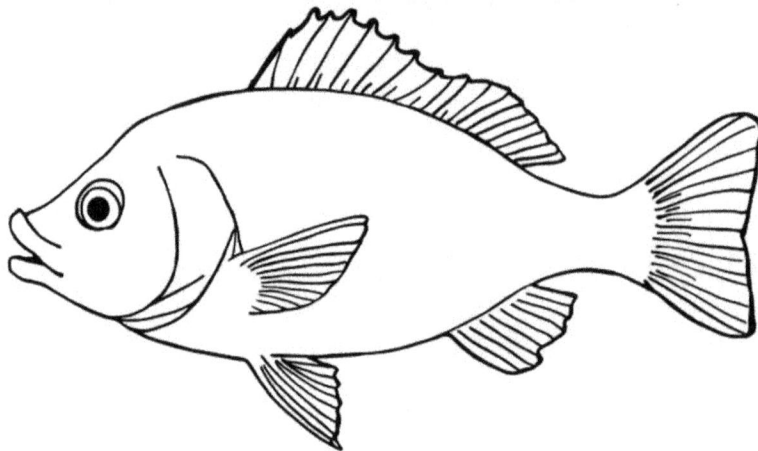

Day Seven: Drawing Prompt (F, T, C)

Task: Copy the drawing prompt below onto a piece of plain paper. Using the subject "a whale of a time," what can you draw while using the prompt as part of your picture? Can you include a background? What will you call your drawing?

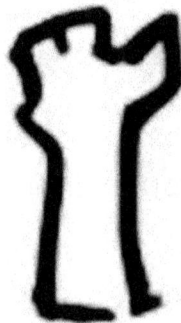

Week Fifty-One Theme: Famous Places

Day One: Design Thinking (F, T, C)
Task: Using only items found around you, can you design and build a 3D model of an actual famous place of your choice? Be sure to come up with a plan first so that you can maximize your time and materials. Also be willing to adjust your plan if needed. How did it turn out? Is it an accurate replica?

Day Two: Fantasy (F, T, C)
Task: Imagine what it would have been like to be alive in a historic place from the past. WHEN and WHERE would you go? WHO would you meet? WHAT would you do? WHY did you make the choice to go where/when you did?

Day Three: Missing Information (F, T, C)
Task: Suppose that you go home today, and the other members of your family are packing their suitcases. When you ask what is going on, the only information you can get is, "We're packing for a trip to the most famous place in the world. Hurry up and pack your suitcase! We have to leave in ten minutes!" What information do you need to know? How will you make sure to be packed and prepared appropriately?

Day Four: Yes, and... (F, T, C)

Task: Using the prompt "If I could visit any famous place, it would be ____, because ____," take turns to complete the sentence. The next person should follow with "Yes, and...." in order to agree and add more details. Continue until everyone has contributed to the line of discussion. Then, someone else will take a turn to complete the prompt with a different place, allowing others to follow with "Yes, and..." statements. How long can you keep the conversation going?

Day Five: Personal Analogy (F, T, C)

Task: Pretend that you are a famous place of your choice. Write a song, story, or poem in the first person about your experiences.

Day Six: Oxymorons (F, T, C)

Task: Oxymorons are phrases that combine two opposite words to convey a new idea. How do you explain some of these oxymorons related to being famous? Can you think of some examples where you might encounter these?

- Famous obscurity
- Unpopular celebrity
- Private celebrity
- Public privacy
- Known secret
- Genuine imitation
- Old news
- Recorded live
- Small crowd
- Working vacation

Week Fifty-One Theme: Famous Places

Day Seven: A Puzzling Situation (F, T, C)

Task: Look at the picture below. What do you suppose is going on here? What details do you notice in the picture? What questions do you have? What do you think happened? What do you think will happen next?

Week Fifty-Two Theme: Beauty

Day One: Observation (F, T, C)
Task: For the day, keep a journal or list of all of the things that you see that represent beauty to you. It could be related to the way someone/something looks, moves, sounds like, or says. At the end of the day, compare lists. Cross off any words or ideas that are identical. Who thought of the most original ideas?

Day Two: Elaboration (F, T, C)
Task: How can you decorate the box below as elaborately as possible? Try to think of as many details as possible.

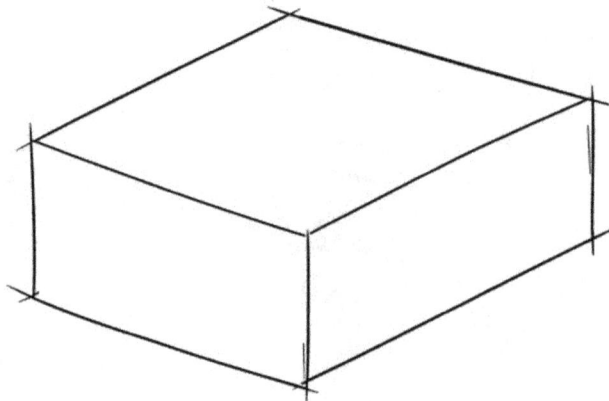

Week Fifty-Two Theme: Beauty

Day Three: Reflection (F, T, C)

Task: If you had to come up with a definition for the word "beauty," what would it be? Do you think that the definition would be different from person to person? Why? What are some things that could influence a person's definition? Do you think that someone/something could change from being an example of beauty to not being one or vice versa? How can that be?

Day Four: Making Judgments (F, T, C)

Task: Looking at the statements below, do you think that they are true or false? Why?

- Beauty is subjective.
- Society dictates what beauty is.
- Beauty is deeper than just physical appearance.
- Beauty is linked to truth.
- Beauty is a promise.
- Beauty is in the eye of the beholder.
- Acceptance of yourself is linked to beauty.
- Being a unique individual is beauty.

Day Five: Museum Walk (F, T, C)

Task: Have each person create a poster about what beauty means. You can create these on your own or cut them out of a magazine. Hang the posters around the room. Have each person rotate to each poster and write/draw responses to either:

- Add more detail
- Ask clarifying or challenging questions
- Agree or disagree

Week Fifty-Two Theme: Beauty

Day Six: Put to a Different Use (F, T, C)
Task: How many different uses can you think of for a mirror besides looking at your reflection?

Day Seven: Drawing Prompt (F, T, C)
Task: Copy the drawing prompt below onto a piece of plain paper. Using the subject "beautiful day," what can you draw while using the prompt as part of your picture? Can you include a background? What will you call your drawing?

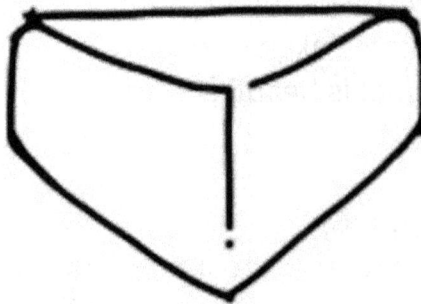

Day 365: Cubism

Task: Gather objects from around you with different shapes. The size of the objects depends on the space you have available and what you would prefer. If you would like to complete this outside on a sidewalk or driveway using chalk, your objects should be on the larger size. If you would like to complete this inside on a large piece of paper, your objects should be on smaller side. Trace the shapes onto your paper either randomly or by making a plan first. What can you turn this into? Think of a theme together and create your masterpiece using simple geometric shapes and collage. Be sure to take some pictures of your masterpiece! What will you call it?

Thank you for reading! I genuinely
hope that you enjoyed it and found it useful.

I would greatly appreciate it if you
would please consider posting a review.

About the Author

Jennifer Bowers has been working in public education for over thirty years, the majority of which have been in gifted education. She holds a Bachelor's degree and Master's degree in Early Childhood Education and an add-on certification in Gifted Education. She has published numerous curriculum units in her school system and has instructed gifted endorsement classes for teachers. She lives in Georgia with her three children and their cats. Her hope in writing this book is to help people grow and bond together while tapping into new challenges.

www.ingramcontent.com/pod-product-compliance
Lightning Source LLC
Chambersburg PA
CBHW081150090426
42736CB00017B/3260